Martin Crimp

Martin Crimp was born in 1956. His plays include *Three Attempted Acts* (1985), *Dealing with Clair* (1988), *Play with Repeats* (1989), *No One Sees the Video* (1991), *Getting Attention* (1992), *The Treatment* (1993, winner of the John Whiting Award), *Attempts on her Life* (1997) and *The Country* (2000). He has translated or adapted work by Ionesco (*The Chairs*, 1997), Koltès (*Roberto Zucco*, 1997), Genet (*The Maids*, 1999) and Molière (*The Misanthrope*, 1996).

His work in the UK has been produced by the Orange Tree Theatre, the West Yorkshire Playhouse, the Stephen Joseph Theatre, the RSC, the Young Vic, Theatre de Complicite and the Royal Court, where he was writer-in-residence in 1997. In New York his work has been seen at the Public Theater and the Classic Stage Company, as well as on Broadway. Of numerous productions in Europe the most recent is *Attempts on her Life* at the Piccolo Teatro in Milan.

MARTIN CRIMP

Plays One

Dealing with Clair
Getting Attention
Play with Repeats
The Treatment

Introduced by
the author

faber and faber

First published in this collection in 2000
by Faber and Faber Limited
3 Queen Square, London WC1N 3AU

Typeset by Country Setting, Kingsdown, Kent CT14 8ES
Printed in England by Mackays of Chatham plc, Chatham, Kent

A CIP record for this book is available from the British Library

ISBN 0–571–20345–0

2 4 6 8 10 9 7 5 3 1

Contents

Four Imaginary Characters

THE THEATRE

The Theatre has strapped me into planes, welcomed me at airports, driven me into strange cities. The Theatre buys me drinks and takes me back to my hotel at 2 a.m. Three hours later it turns on a bright lamp close to my eyes, tells me to wake up and vomit.

The Theatre has dinner with me in a quiet restaurant beside the water of Hamburg's Aussenalster, or coffee in a Florence suburb. It passes me a microphone. It asks me to speak. It amplifies my voice. It flies me to New York where by early evening the second hand of my watch has started jumping under the glass like an insect. Outside the rich, glittering party a taxi is waiting in the February rain to take me straight to Bucharest where the loose dollars in my trouser-pocket are enough to pay my host's salary for a month. The Theatre shows me glowing brickwork broken open by bullets. 'Where you are standing,' it says, 'the street ran with blood.'

It likes me to meet the actors. We go into the hospital-like labyrinth and knock on their doors. Each one opens onto the same bright scene: the actors swivelling away from their mirrors and lamps, their tissues, polystyrene cups, postcards, messages, flowers, ashtrays, to see who's coming in. 'Oh my god – so you're the writer!' The room becomes a tiny theatre in which we improvise delight, modesty, anxiety, mutual respect, with varying degrees of success.

THE WRITER

One night, in a wide bed, I can hear breathing. I'm terrified, because I should be alone. My body goes rigid as I listen, until I realize that what I can hear is probably the coolant churning in the refrigerator. I turn over in the bed to face the other way and go back to sleep, and that's when I discover the Writer. He's lying beside me, smiling, his eyes wide open and black, like the aperture of a camera. It's an unpleasant surprise. And when I ask him what he thinks he's doing, just what he thinks he's doing in my bed, his answer is not reassuring. 'I've come to spend my life with you,' he says. He goes on to explain that certain people, certain people like myself, are selected to be inhabited by writers. I'm not sure I like this word 'inhabited'. 'What do you mean?' 'Well,' says the Writer, 'we writers identify people who have nothing inside, who are dead inside – if you'll pardon me saying so – and we move into them the way a hermit crab moves into an empty shell.' 'What makes you think I'm dead inside?' I ask. 'Why else would I be here?' says the Writer, stroking my cheek. This is clearly a bad dream. I roll away from his repulsive finger and fall deeply asleep. In the morning I'm alone again, thank god, only there's this faint buzzing sound coming from the bathroom. I push open the door: it's the Writer. And what's more, he's using my electric toothbrush.

The first thing he does is rearrange my furniture. He drags a table over to the window to write at. He rips up the carpet ('suburban') so he can pace the boards in his big ugly boots. He mocks my alphabetical rows of books ('anal') and tips his own out of their boxes straight onto the floor. He makes fun of my beautiful old piano ('bourgeois') acquired at great expense, and during his

brutal, tuneless improvisations ('tonality is dead'),
delights in leaving his cigarettes burning on the finely
veined keys. What made me think that writers were quiet
and sensitive? Everything he does is coarse, crude and
vicious. And I'm expected to mirror all his moods. When
he's at the window doing his precious writing, I have to
be completely silent ('turn off that television or I'll
fucking kill you'). When he wants to go out, I have to
keep up with his drinking, laugh at his cynical jokes,
even collude in his desperate womanising. But the very
worst is having to sit up half the night tending his
bottomless self-pity which he refers to, rather more
gloriously, as 'anguish' or 'despair'. Compared to this,
my other duties are fairly straightforward: answering the
phone, cutting his long white hair.

When he goes out on his own for cigarettes or eggs
I have a chance to catch up on the housework. I change
the sheets, hoover up as much ash and bitten fingernail
as I can, and try to make neat piles of the books. Some
of these are his – I mean in the sense that the Writer
wrote them – doubly his, in fact. And look: there's his
picture on the flap. I wonder how many rolls of film they
got through before they came up with an image that was
acceptably human?

I'm sometimes asked what I think of the Writer's
work, especially now he's apparently making something
of a name for himself. But why should the shell show
any interest in the scribblings of the crab? I've heard a
few things about what he gets up to, flicked through a
few pages, and it doesn't sound like my kind of thing,
quite frankly. How can someone who spends so many
hours watching the trees change colour, or children
skipping, come up with all that pain and brutality? Isn't
it perverse? I may be dead inside, but if I sat at that
window I know I'd see the world in a very different

light. I wouldn't mock or rage. I'd keep it simple. I'd spend a whole day, a whole week if I had to, trying to describe the trajectory of a falling leaf – or the way that a child, unlike an adult, will break into a run simply for pleasure.

THE DIRECTOR

One night, on the way home from the theatre, the Director decides to call me. Over the past year I've tried to get in touch a number of times. At first the phone just rang and rang, but as the months went by the ringing stopped and was replaced by an automated message – *kein Anschluss* – no connection. This was mysterious not just because the Director, an old friend, seemed to have vanished from the face of the earth, but also because the word *Anschluss* was used for the annexation of Austria, which is where the Director now lives. The Director is a big man, arrogant and warm. When you meet him, he wraps his arms around you and his stubble scratches your cheek.

'I'm walking home,' he says, 'I've been very busy.' Busy? This doesn't seem quite adequate for a year's silence. I try to picture the busy Director walking home through the streets of his city at night, but my imagination, not for the first time, fails. All I can see is the Danube on a Sunday morning – or no, it must be a weekday, because the miniature train with its quaint and beautifully restored wooden interior *the steepest track railway in Europe* is taking schoolchildren home to their immaculate hillside suburbs which face, to the south, a disused concentration camp. At five hundred and thirty-seven metres the train reaches its upper terminus where narrow roads strewn with leaves spiral round a church with two towers. It's October. The restaurants and terraces designed to absorb

the beautiful broad view of the river look closed, but in
fact they're simply empty. The light is yellow and low.
The trees look lit from the wings.

However banal you find the idea of 'coincidence', you
have to admit it's odd that the Director should choose
this moment to call, just when the introduction to these
plays has to be written, because the picture on the cover
is a photograph from one of his own productions.
'What are you going to write?' he says, knowing full
well this question has the same effect on me as the sound
of a dentist's drill and the spatter of pulped tooth on the
protective goggles. 'I've no idea,' I say, 'maybe something
about the way plays are like children – part of you is
printed into every cell of their bodies, you go on feeling
responsible for them – but the fact is they're separate
entities leading separate lives. What do you think?'
'You know, Martin,' says the Director as he walks home
through his well-lit reconstructed streets, 'I think you
should steer clear of that kind of metaphorical stuff.
You don't mind me saying this, do you?' 'No, of course
not. Absolutely.' 'What people want is a flavour of what
it's like to write plays – not a flavour of the plays
themselves, because hopefully the plays will do that job
for you – just put your reader inside your head for a
little while.' 'Inside my head.' 'Inside your head, that's
right. Give them a little tour.'

THE ACTOR

The Writer has paused in front of a shop-window in a
sunny thoroughfare. In the shop-window, behind bars,
there's a display of alarm-clocks, the kind with two bells
on the top and a beater between them. The Writer is
so taken by this spectacle of the clocks that he doesn't
notice the Actor until she appears beside him and speaks.

'It's difficult for us to believe that you exist.' The Actor isn't smiling when she says this – or if she is – and yes, in fact she is – quite possibly she is – but if she is, then it's the serious, occluded smile of someone whose life, unlike the Writer's, has been scarred by the corrosive apparatus of control and secrecy which is now being painfully dismantled.

The Writer is about to make a witty reply about his own existence, or existence in general, or worse still some trivial comment about the funny-looking clocks, but he checks himself when he meets the Actor's eyes, when he remembers the room in the theatre where she and the other actors live, sleeping on mattresses on the floor.

Martin Crimp
October 1999

DEALING WITH CLAIR

Dealing with Clair was first performed at the Orange Tree Theatre, Richmond, by arrangement with Michael Codron, on 14 October 1988, with the following cast:

Mike John Michie
Liz Julia Hills
Clair Janine Wood
James Tom Courtenay
Anna Anna Mazzotti
Ashley, Vittorio, Toby Matthew Sim

Director Sam Walters
Designer Anne Gruenberg

Characters

James, fifties, a cash buyer

Mike, thirty ⎱
Liz, thirty ⎰ the vendors

Clair, twenty-five, negotiator to the vendors
Anna, seventeen, the vendors' Italian nanny
Ashley, twenty-five, a tradesman
Vittorio, twenty-two, a friend of Anna
Toby, twenty-five, a colleague of Clair

The place is London, the time the end of the 1980s,
the month August – with the exception of the final scene,
which takes place in October of the same year

There are three locations:

1 A room in the vendors' house. Doorways to hall
and kitchen. A tall sash window faces north

2 Clair's flat. A small studio room

3 The vendors' garden

Note

A comma on a separate line indicates a pause,
the exact duration of which must be determined
from the context.

Act One

SCENE ONE

Darkness.
The sound of a high-speed train approaching. As it reaches maximum, the light comes up to reveal Clair talking on the phone at night in her tiny flat. The train passes right outside the window. Only as it recedes can we hear her speak.

Clair . . . Simply that we are in the middle of it and so of course there's a certain amount of aggression which we must *deal* with. We must deal with it but
Aggression, aggression, aggression not
Aggression, *not violence.* Simply simply
Please listen to me: *not violence,* simply that that that people's yes their feelings *are* aroused, their feelings are naturally aroused and so it is a strain, it is a stress, yes, to deal, undeniably, to deal with people, *yes. But*
That
That
That is what I enjoy. That is what I am good at, OK?

Sound of a train approaching. She raises her voice.

I'm not *angry.* I'm not *angry,* I'm just trying to *explain.* OK, I *sound* angry, but I'm *not* angry, I'm just trying to explain one or two things, one or two things about

The train passes, making it momentarily impossible to speak.

one or two things about *what?* (*Laughs.*)
What young man? What young man? Come on, come on, there is no 'young man'.

7

Toby? (*Laughs.*) Toby is history. I will never forgive him for what happened in the restaurant.

What? Didn't I tell you? Didn't I tell you what happened in the restaurant? The *bill*? OK, there's what? six of us? eight of us? in this smart Italian place (are you sure I didn't tell you about this?)

OK, and we're celebrating opening the new office (because suddenly we've got new offices opening *every*where – it's insane) and anyway

Anyway, when the bill comes the assumption quite naturally is that we will divide it, we will divide it by six or by eight or by however many of us there are.

Exactly. But then Toby, Toby, Toby starts this business where he says that the two of *us* (as if we're some kind of married couple) that the two of *us* have had less than the others.

Exactly. Of course it's not appropriate. But he asks for the menu back and he makes (can you believe this?) makes everyone calculate their own separate totals at which point I want to

Well exactly: die. And of course the separate totals no way do they add up to the exact amount on the bill. But he won't let it rest, he just goes on and on and on about who drank this, who ate that

Sound of train approaching. She raises her voice.

who had coffee, who *didn't* have coffee. And the worst thing is that I am drawn into this, I am sucked into this, because Toby is implicating me in this mad mad mad, this mad . . . *thing.*

The train passes. Clair rummages in her bag.

Yup, yup, yup, of course I'm listening. I'm just looking for I'm just looking for

No I am not 'looking for a cigarette'. You know I've given up. (*She produces a cigarette.*) Yes, I *promise* you

8

I've given up. I'm just – one moment . . . (*She turns away and lights the cigarette.*) . . . I'm just looking for . . . my diary. I thought I'd lost my diary. But it's right here . . . in my bag.

I am not lying. I know it kills you. And that's why I've stopped, OK? (*brightly*) Listen, did I tell you I've decorated?

That's right. Bank holiday Monday. I've done the whole place in a kind of . . . (*looks round the room*) a kind of . . . well I suppose it's what you'd call neutral, it's not really a colour, it's a kind of nothing, just a kind of nothing sort of *what*?

Live with it? I *won't be* living with it.

Yes I *know* I've only just bought it, but I didn't buy it to *live* in it, I bought it to *sell* it, as you well know. And anyway, what's wrong with neutral?

A pause. Clair seems to withdraw from the phone call. A train passes, but faintly in the distance.

Sorry. I was dreaming. What?

Well I *know* you and Dad wouldn't've thought that way. I *know* you were grateful just to have a home. I *know* you had to economise. I *know* you had to make sacrifices but the world's just not like that any more. Why *should* we make sacrifices? Sacrifices for what? I don't have anyone to make sacrifices *for*, and I certainly don't intend to sacrifice *myself* thank you very much. *And* I happen to be very happy with my life.

Well I'm sorry. I'm sorry if I don't sound happy. Just tell me what 'happy' sounds like – OK? (*She laughs – and has clearly made Mum laugh.*) Well exactly. And besides, it's not for ever.

Selling houses. It's not for ever. Who knows *what* I'll do? Maybe make a killing and just . . . disappear.

(*Laughs.*) That's right. Vanish.

Sound of a train approaching. Clair goes to the window.

(*Laughs.*) Of *course* you can come too. I'll buy you both a mansion on the beach.

Exactly: right next to the water.

All that sand and blue sea. (*She laughs and turns to the window.*)

At the moment of the train's maximum impact: blackout.

The rush and whine of the train continues – finally fading away as the light comes up on the next scene.

SCENE TWO

A room in the vendors' house. Morning.

Clair stands exactly as in the previous scene, in front of a tall window, her back turned.

Mike stands on the other side of the room, looking at her.

After a long silence, she senses his look and turns. Both smile.

Mike Look, I'm sorry, I haven't shown you the garden.

Clair I don't think I need to go out there.

Mike I'm afraid it faces north.

Clair Yes, but it's a garden.

Both faint laugh.

The plant along the wall . . .

Mike Yes, that's a vine.

Clair Right, that's good. Vines are a good feature.

Mike Yes, that's why we put it in, I'm afraid. Because we liked it as it was, but we've tried to do as much as we can out there with an eye to selling.

Clair The slabs.

Mike Yes, I put down those slabs.

,

I'm afraid it's never had any fruit.

Clair Well . . . (*irrelevant*)

Mike I'm not sure what we'd do with it if it did. We're not gardeners, are you?

Clair You're joking.

Both faint laugh.

May I ask how long you've been here?

Mike It's a couple of years now. Well that's what we planned. I think any longer than that in one place and unfortunately you just start to tread water.

Clair Well, in the present climate . . .

Mike That's right.

,

So.

Clair Well I think we're probably looking at about a hundred and seventy-five.

Mike A hundred and seventy-five.

Clair I think we could try it.

Mike Right.

,

Clair You're not happy with that.

Mike We'd actually like to try a hundred and ninety.

Clair A hundred and ninety.

Mike Well I think so, don't you.

Clair You know Number Five went recently.

Mike And that was how much?

Clair One-seventy.

Mike One-seventy, when was that?

Clair It's a month or so now. Of course people are achieving some very good prices with these older properties. And this is a good road.

Mike Of course a lot of it was tenants.

Clair Yes, but that's changing.

Mike Mind you it's quite disgusting what's happening to the tenants.

'

You know we've got four bedrooms here.

Clair Well yes, you've got a –

Mike That's right, because most of these properties only have three. Number Five only has three.

Clair It doesn't have a window, does it.

Mike It doesn't have a window as such, but it's a good size. We've put our Italian girl in there actually. She loves the atmosphere. I mean here. In England. She's from Naples.

Clair But not the room.

Mike I'm sorry?

,

No, she's very pleased with the room. It's the first time she's had her own room.

,

Clair A hundred and ninety.

Mike Well I think we could give it a try, don't you?

Clair It's pushing it.

Mike (*faint laugh*) Well I know.

Clair But of course people are getting away with it.

Mike Well I know. That's the thing. People are – unfortunately – getting away with it, as you say. And so, well, you see our dilemma. I mean I know the whole thing's hateful.

Clair Well . . .

Mike But look what I mean is, is assuming we can get it, assuming we can get this price, because actually I think it's a perfectly realistic price, but assuming we can achieve that, well obviously we'd like to behave honourably in this if you see what I mean.

Clair I'm sorry, how's that?

Mike Well what I mean is, is I simply mean I think strictly first come first served, don't you, as far as any offers are concerned.

Clair Well yes, if that's how you feel.

Mike Well don't you think that's right.

Clair Well yes, of course, if that's how you feel, yes. Of course what we'd normally do is advise you to accept the best offer we receive, I mean with regard not just to the price, but taking into account who's in the best position to exchange.

Mike Yes. Well actually that's just the kind of thing I mean.

Clair Because naturally we try to do what's best for our clients.

Mike Well yes. I see that.

,

Clair But of course it's absolutely up to you.

Mike Right.

,

Clair I mean if someone comes along with cash.

Mike Right.

Clair That's all I mean.

,

Well we'll get the details out as soon as we can, Mr Walsum.

Mike Mike, it's Mike.

Clair Mike. Fine.

She's about to go.

Mike You don't live near the Green, do you Clair?

Clair I'm sorry?

Mike I'm sorry, it is Clair isn't it.

Clair Yes.

Mike I say: you don't live near the Green.

14

Clair (*on the word 'near'*) No. I'm further north.

Mike It's only a girl crossed the road in front of my car down there. At the lights. I'm sure it was you.

Clair (*faint laugh*) I must look like somebody else.

Mike Surely not.

That this is intended as a compliment is not lost on Clair.
  Liz is standing in the doorway.

Right. Good. Clair.

Mike and Clair shake hands.

Liz So everything's settled, is it?

Mike Fine, it's fine.

Liz He has told you how we feel, hasn't he?

Mike Yes, yes it's fine. What, is she asleep?

Liz Just gone.

Clair She's lovely.

Liz She's lovely when she's asleep. No, it's just that we want to behave honourably in this.

Clair Mr Walsum's told me your position.

Liz Because it's a hateful business.

Clair No. Of course. It's absolutely up to you.

Liz Has she seen the garden?

Clair I've seen it from the window.

Liz I'm afraid we're not gardeners, are we.

,

Clair Have you found somewhere?

Liz Actually we're going to take a flat, aren't we.

Mike Of course it will mean being on top of each other for a while.

Liz Yes, it's going to be a little difficult . . .

Mike What with Anna . . .

Liz Well even without Anna, Mike. Because really it's very small. But we'll have the advantage of being cash.

Clair You'll be in a good position.

Liz Well yes, we will. And of course we'll be less pressured . . .

Mike We want to take our time over this one.

Liz Because we have some friends of ours . . .

Mike Poppy and Max . . .

Liz . . . who panicked completely and ended up living on a railway, didn't they Mike.

They all laugh.

Clair Of course it's not necessarily a bad investment.

Mike Yes, but they're horribly overlooked, aren't they.

Clair Listen, will you want to leave a key with us?

Liz Well I think we should, don't you.

Mike I can drop one round.

Liz (*laughs*) Just make sure no one sees the stain.

Mike That's right. Steer them clear of the stain.

Clair I'm sorry? The stain? What is that?

Liz I think you're standing on it actually.

Clair faint laugh, looks down, moves a little.

Clair Right. I'll . . . I'll try to avoid the stain. We'll get the details out as soon as we can.

Clair moves off. Mike follows.
A baby's crying.

Liz Anna. (*louder*) Anna, she's awake.

She goes to the hall doorway and calls.

Anna, she's awake.

She's about to go out, when the crying stops.
Mike returns.

Mike What is it?

Liz She's awake.

Mike Won't Anna go?

Liz She just has.

They embrace.

So she's agreed on one-ninety.

Mike She didn't want to. She knew about Number Five.

Liz But it's only got three bedrooms.

Mike I told her that.

,

Sweet, isn't she?

Liz What?

Mike Clair.

Liz Is she? (*She moves away.*)

Look, I'd better go.

Mike Hasn't Anna gone?

Liz It's her day off.

Mike She doesn't mind. Look, d'you want a coffee? Liz?

But Liz has gone.
Mike goes into the kitchen. The stage is empty for a moment.
Then Anna, the Italian girl, appears in a dressing-gown. She approaches the telephone, but seems uncertain about using it.
Mike reappears.

Mike Good morning.

,

Do we have a problem?

Anna Is alright if I telephone, Mr Walsum?

Mike Provided it's not Australia. (*faint laugh*)

Anna Sorry?

Mike I say: as long as it's not Australia.

Anna No no. Italy.

,

Mike Fine. That's fine.

Anna You don't mind?

Mike Italy is absolutely fine. Just keep it short please. (*He doesn't move.*)

Anna My family.

Mike No no, that's fine. Please go ahead. Just keep it short, that's all. (*He returns to the kitchen.*)

Anna dials, waits, waits some more, hangs up and is about to leave when Mike reappears with coffee.

Well you were quick.

Anna Is no one there.

Mike What, in the whole of Italy? (*Laughs.*)

Anna I'm sorry?

,

Mike Look, has someone, well I mean you actually, you haven't, you haven't been smoking upstairs have you? It's just Mrs Walsum – Liz – Liz thought she could smell smoke up there, that's all, the other day I think it was.

Anna I don't smoke, Mr Walsum.

Mike Well no no, I know you don't. Well that's fine then, naturally.

Anna If I may try later on.

Mike By all means.

,

Look, we've been wondering if we've, well if we've been giving you enough spending money. Because, well, it isn't really very much.

Anna No no. It's fine.

Mike You're managing.

Anna I'm managing.

Mike Well I'm very pleased to hear you're managing because as you probably know, what with moving, and renting the flat, things are going to get a little tight. And I mean I don't want you to think we're the sort of people who like to . . . (*vague gesture*) . . . well exploit this kind of situation. Because I know some people do with –

well particularly with foreign girls they tend to take advantage.

,

Because you know – well *obviously* you know we're not like that.

Anna I'm managing. Thank you.

Mike Listen, can I get you a coffee or anything?

,

Fine. Well. Anyway, you know where it is. (*Mike lingers a moment more, then starts to go. At the last moment he turns.*)

Look, I was just thinking, perhaps you ought to get dressed. It's just that people – hopefully – people – will be coming round to view.

Anna (*with complete indifference*) OK.

Mike I mean you know we don't mind on your day off. It's just that, well you just can't tell what's going to put people off unfortunately.

Anna OK.

Mike Not that you would, obviously, put people off. I mean you wouldn't put *me* off. But just in case somebody should come, please.

Anna OK, that's OK.

Mike Thanks, Anna.

> Mike starts to go. At the last moment he stops as before and looks at Anna. She senses his look and turns.

Thanks.

> He goes.
> Blackout.

SCENE THREE

Evening. Mike and Liz.

Liz No objections to doing what?

Mike To leaving it on.

Liz But you told her we'd accept and were prepared to wait.

Mike Yes yes I said we accept but Clair's feeling is in case for whatever reason – because of course people do – they happen to drop out, or I don't know find it difficult to exchange, there's no harm in leaving it on. And besides I felt she was implying –

Liz Because I thought we'd both talked to her about this.

Mike Well of course, but I felt she was implying that if we got more interest we could, there would be the possibility that we could maybe push them up.

Liz You told her we weren't prepared to do that.

Mike Well she already knows we wouldn't do that.

,

It was something I made clear in our first conversation.

Liz (*on 'conversation'*) How far up?

Mike What?

Liz All I mean is –

Mike I don't know. She was vague.

,

Two hundred?

Liz As far as that.

Mike She seemed to think we could be looking at another five to ten thou, yes.

'

Liz Well that's hardly significant.

Mike Well no, I agree it's not particularly significant in the present climate – well five wouldn't be certainly, although perhaps ten . . . But the point is, and this is surely what we're talking about, is if it goes under offer like this in less than forty-eight hours, then maybe we're simply not asking enough.

Liz This is what Clair said?

Mike Well it's not what she *said*, no.

'

It's not what she *said* but here we are, here we are, we're paying them x per cent, and how much work will they actually have *done*?

'

It's complicated you see by the fact that these people, the Harraps, are in Shropshire.

Liz You mean they might not be genuine.

Mike Genuine or whatever, I just mean there's a question mark over their ability to sell. Because, as Clair said, if they're stuck up there in Wales . . .

Liz England.

Mike England.

'

Is it?

Liz I think it is.

Mike Well wherever it is.

Liz Shrewsbury.

Mike Well wherever it is there's not much of a market.

Liz Just sheep.

Mike That sort of thing.

Mike lies with his head in Liz's lap.

They've got several acres up there according to Clair.
A stream. Fishing rights. You drive up through a pine . . .
some kind of pine . . . *thing*. Forest.

Liz It's rural.

Mike That's right. I mean it's not something I'd
personally go along with, but surely if they've got that
much land they'd keep it and build on it.

Liz It must be protected.

Mike (*faint laugh*) Clair says she's got a crumbly spine.

Liz A what?

Mike Mrs Harrap. They're moving on account of her
spine.

Liz What, are they old?

Mike No, they're like us apparently.

Liz And they don't mind the garden?

Mike Apparently they've fallen in love with the garden.
They were very taken by the vine.

Liz So you've had a long chat with Clair.

,

23

Mike What's that supposed to mean?

Liz But you made it clear we're prepared to wait.

Mike Listen: Clair knows exactly what we've said to her and I'm sure she respects our position.

Liz Meaning.

Mike What d'you mean, meaning?

Liz Well meaning what?

Mike What do I mean by meaning?

Liz What do you mean by position, respects our position?

Mike Well exactly what I say.

Liz Which is?

Mike What?

Liz Well what exactly *are* you saying?

Mike Because if I have to explain myself every time I speak . . .

Liz Because it seems to me, and of course maybe I'm wrong, but it seems to me you're saying you're deferring to Clair.

Mike I've no intention of deferring to Clair. Come on, come on. It's simply that since we find ourselves dealing with her, then perhaps – well no, not perhaps – I think we *should* I really think we should show at least some respect for her judgement and integrity.

Liz Her *what*? (*faint laugh*)

'

So you're deferring to Clair.

Mike Look, I'm not deferring to Clair. She's deferring to us.

Liz (*amused*) D'you think she always wears that skirt?

Mike What?

Liz Well she looks like a waitress.

Both faint laugh.
Blackout.

SCENE FOUR

Morning. Clair stands at the window, back turned.
James stands on the other side of the room, looking at her.
She senses his look and turns. Both smile.

James There's a good atmosphere here, isn't there? Very calm and quiet. I think that's very valuable, don't you. Because while I could never imagine living outside of a city, still I like a home to be a kind of sanctuary. Do you know it's rather like when you drive off the road, isn't it. Because you know how it is when you drive off the road onto one of those gravel tracks that leads into a mountain forest. The Pyrenees for example, the French Pyrenees. You drive slowly between the trees, then a little way in you turn off the engine. Then it strikes you. The silence.

,

Do you suppose it's the light? Perhaps it's the quality of the light here. That window faces north, doesn't it?

Clair Yes, I think so.

James Because quite frankly I'm much happier with reflected light. Whenever I have to go a long way south

25

I'm afraid I tend to languish rather. If I don't have a marble floor I can get very irritable. (*with equal charm*) You do realise that sill is rotten, don't you. I could get my finger in up to the knuckle.

Both faint laugh.

James (*with attack*) Bedroom four.

Clair Yes?

James Have I missed bedroom four?

Clair It's the room with the pictures.

James What, those views of Naples?

Clair Are they?

James Well aren't they? It doesn't have a window, does it. Is that why it smells of smoke?

Clair It's actually quite a good size.

James Well do you know I thought it was a cupboard. I thought, well that's odd, I've stumbled into a cupboard with views of Naples. (*faint laugh*)

Clair What's the position with your own property?

James Position in what sense?

Clair I mean is your own house sold?

James I think we're at cross purposes. No, I'm not selling any houses. I think that's a hateful business, selling houses. No, I simply wish to acquire a new one here in London. Because do you know I suddenly felt terribly lost at Heathrow the other day. I drove to a hotel but my heart wasn't in it. That's when I thought, I need something of my own here after all these years. I'm fed up with hotels, Clair, and so is my family. We're fed up with hotels here in London. I think that's a desolate kind of life, don't you.

Clair You travel on business.

James I travel a lot on business.

,

Clair So you're in a good position.

James Well I think I am, don't you?

Both faint laugh.

The thing is, is it's an elegant house. Parts of it have obviously been abused, but underneath there is an elegant house.

Clair Anything in this road is a good investment.

James Well I'm sure it is, but frankly that's not what concerns me.

,

You say in fact it's sold.

Clair The vendors have accepted an offer.

James The vendors have accepted an offer.

Clair Yes, but if someone matches it with cash.

James And what is the offer?

Clair The asking price.

James Which is? I'm sorry, I . . .

Clair A hundred and ninety.

James And who wishes to purchase?

Clair The Harraps.

James Do I know them?

Clair I'm sorry?

James Who are the Harraps?

Clair Well, well they're just . . .

James They're just people you mean.

Clair Well they're in Shropshire.

James Whereabouts is that?

Clair Isn't it Wales?

James I mean whereabouts in Shropshire. Because I know Shropshire. I used to know Shrewsbury well.

Clair Would you like to see the garden?

James You know, I don't think there's any need, do you? Because I like what I've seen very much, Clair.

Clair I'm afraid it faces north, but there's a vine.

James We're not gardeners.

Both faint laugh. Silence.

James (*with a laugh*) There's a certain kind of man who would exploit this kind of situation. I mean if I were to make an offer . . .

Clair We'd put it to the vendors.

James You'd put it to the vendors.

Clair Well naturally.

James Because I should stress I like what I've seen very much.

Clair Well I'm sure they'd consider it.

James I really think I ought to meet them, don't you? We ought to talk. Because naturally I want to behave honourably in this, Clair.

Clair I'll speak to the Walsums.

James Are they Dutch?

Clair I don't think so.

James Because Walsum is Dutch.

Clair moves away to check everything is undisturbed prior to leaving.

James Do you know I saw a girl like you when I was on my way here.

Clair Did you? (*faint laugh*)

James (*laughs*) I'm sorry, I'm embarrassing you.

Clair laughs.

Or perhaps it *was* you. Was it you?

Clair I don't know.

,

Look, I'll try and fix up that appointment.

James Would you. Listen, I'm sorry about that.

Clair It's alright.

James I mean when I called you a girl. Because it's one of those words, isn't it, it's one of those dreadful words men use to belittle women. It's funny isn't it, how you are terribly aware of everybody else's faults, and then you find you share them too. I apologise.

Clair It's alright.

James Because please understand I hate that sort of thing as much as you must.

Clair (*as if to go*) Well look, I'll try and fix up that appointment.

James Would you? My wife will love it. The children will love that garden.

Clair How many do you have?

James What did I say? Did I say children? No, just the one. (*He takes out a wallet and shows it to Clair.*) Marcus. A boy.

Clair looks at the picture.

Well hardly my boy. He's my wife's boy.

,

Clair She must be –

James Considerably younger. Yes, she is. But what about you, Clair. Are you married? Single? Surely not widowed? Divorced?

Clair begins to laugh during this. They both laugh for a while.

Children?

Clair You're joking. (*She gives back the wallet. Silence. She fiddles with the keys, almost as if she has temporarily withdrawn into a private world.*)

James I'll tell you something – and of course I may be completely wrong – but why is it I have an idea you live on a railway. Is that right?

Clair (*faint laugh*) Yes. Yes I do.

James I thought you did.

,

Isn't that odd. You see I imagine you in one of those rooms right on the railway. I see you in one of those tall old houses turned into flats, where the track passes on

30

brick arches right outside the upper windows. If you go by at night you often have a glimpse down into these rooms. You can see people acting in a very ordinary way, as if there was no train outside. Often the light bulbs have no shades. Isn't that odd. But then how else are they supposed to act?

Clair A lot of people live on railways.

James Well of course they do. Does your bulb have a shade?

Clair It's not necessarily a bad investment.

James Well of course not.

,

Those are the keys?

Clair Yes. (*She snaps them shut in her fist.*) We'd better go.

James Absolutely.

Blackout.

SCENE FIVE

Evening. Mike and Liz.

Liz No objections to doing what?

Mike To leaving it on.

Liz But you told her we'd accept and were prepared to wait.

Mike Yes yes yes, but that was before this. That was before we were talking about cash.

Liz So you've spoken to Clair.

Mike Well obviously I've spoken to Clair.

,

I mean Clair seems to think –

Liz So what's his position?

Mike The position *is*, as I understand it is, is he likes what he's seen very much and he's prepared to pay cash.

Liz So he's already sold, but do we *know* he's already sold?

Mike No no no, he's nothing to sell.

,

The whole point is, is that he has nothing to sell.

Liz (*on 'nothing'*) Well it's easy enough to say that. We could say that.

Mike What, you don't think he's honest?

Liz I've not 'spoken to Clair'.

Mike Well I've told you her opinion.

Liz Is that what she said?

Mike Is what what she said?

Liz What?

Mike Is what what she said?

Liz That in her opinion he's honest.

Mike Because look, it's impossible for me, please understand it's impossible for me to relate to you word for word exactly what she said.

Liz Word for word, no one said word for word, I just –

Mike Well whatever.

Liz I've never said word for word.

Mike Well whatever, Liz. Because listen, you talk to her . . .

Liz I'm not talking to her . . .

Mike Because if you talked to her you'd find out the simple fact is, is you don't go round asking if people are honest because that's not ultimately what's at issue here. What's at issue is his ability to exchange.

Liz Which is exactly the same thing.

Mike Well of course it's not.

,

Well listen of course it isn't. Because even if he's not (*gesture of inverted commas*) 'honest', whatever that actually means, meaning I suppose he's still in reality got somewhere to sell, who's to say he won't in spite of that be able to complete faster than the Harraps, who let's face it have saddled themselves with this crumbling ancestral home or spine or whatever it is surrounded by acres of land of outstanding natural beauty but no commercial value whatsoever.

Silence.

Anyway, look, he wants to take another look round.

Liz When?

Mike Tonight. He's coming tonight.

Liz You could've said.

Mike Well he wants his wife to see it.

,

Is Anna dressed?

33

Liz Well how do I know if she's dressed?

Mike I would just rather she was dressed.

Liz Did you ask her about smoking?

Mike Because the way she wanders around here . . .
What? No. She doesn't. I've *told* you she doesn't.

Liz I'm just worried about –

Mike About the Harraps. Look –

Liz Because we've accepted their offer.

Mike Yes but what does that mean? Legally it means
nothing.

,

Liz Well legally it means nothing, but –

Mike You have to remember there's always been a
question mark over the Harraps.

,

Liz I suppose they'd do it if they were in our position.

Mike In their position they'd be even more likely to.

,

Don't you see? Even more likely to. Because, alright,
we may have scruples about this, but it doesn't mean
that they have. Do we know them? We don't even know
who they are. And it seems absurd to put ourselves
under some kind of obligation to a couple of complete
strangers.

,

I mean I'll be frank, I get the impression Clair finds all
this rather amusing.

Liz You mean she's laughing at us?

,

Mike Well can you blame her? Because I think we're
tending to blow this up into some kind of moral issue
when there isn't in fact a moral issue here at all.

Doorbell. They drop their voices.

Liz Well we've never said it's a moral issue.

Mike Well that's right. (*He moves off.*)

Liz The stain.

Mike What?

Liz Give me time to cover the stain.

Mike goes. Liz attempts to cover the stain.
Mike returns with James.

Mike And this is my wife.

James Hello.

Liz Hello. I'm Liz.

James I'm late. I do apologise.

They shake hands. A slight pause.

Liz Well . . . Look . . .

Mike Please . . .

Liz Just go wherever you like.

James I'd quite like to take another look upstairs if
I may.

Liz Well fine, that would be fine.

Mike Is Gina asleep?

Liz Yes, there's a baby asleep up there.

James I shan't make a sound.

Liz Where's Anna?

Mike Yes, there's our Italian girl. Well isn't she in her room?

James Well in that case I'll . . .

Liz No no. You don't need to worry. Go straight in.

Mike (*laughs*) She's getting used to it.

James Which room is that?

Liz Well we think of it as the guest room, don't we Mike.

Mike Of course it's internally lit.

James Yes, there's no window in there, is there.

Mike Not a window as such, but it's actually quite a good size.

Liz Anna rather likes the privacy.

James Yes, but I was thinking of air.

Liz Oh, she has plenty of air, doesn't she Mike.

Mike Air is not a problem.

Liz (*faint laugh*) She certainly seems to breathe.

Mike She definitely breathes. She is constantly in fact . . . breathing.

'

James Well anyway I'll knock.

James goes out.

Liz (*sotto voce*) I thought he was bringing his wife.

,

Mike (*sotto voce*) I'd better unlock the back door. (*He moves off.*)

Liz Mike.

Mike He'll want to see the garden. (*He goes.*)

Liz alone. Time passes. She goes over to the dark window.
    James enters.

James Isn't she lovely. How old is she?

Liz Seventeen.

James I mean your little girl.

Liz (*faint laugh*) She's six months.

James Six months. Isn't that lovely. Do you know I think she has your eyes.

Liz We were expecting your wife.

James She trusts my judgement.

Liz Isn't she curious?

James No.

Both faint laugh.

There's a good atmosphere here isn't there. It's very calm and quiet. I was saying to Clair it reminds me of driving off the road. I mean one of those gravel tracks that takes you into a forest. The sound of the crushed gravel is quite shocking. But when you finally stop between the trees and turn off the engine, it immediately strikes you. The silence. And as you walk away from the gravel you make no sound at all on the decaying needles. Do you know the Pyrenees at all, the French Pyrenees?

37

Liz What, do you travel on business?

James I travel a lot on business.

Liz Which is?

James Pictures. I deal in pictures.

Liz Oh. Is that interesting?

James Well I like it.

,

Liz Yes, we like France, but it's getting so expensive.

James I know. France is expensive. I have a little house there. It's hardly much bigger than this actually. But I've had the floors replaced and it's costing me a fortune. Most of the year I'm not even there.

Liz Would you like to see the garden?

James Well I don't think I need to, do you Liz. It is Liz, isn't it. Well I don't think I need to, Liz.

Liz I suppose it's dark.

James Well exactly.

Mike appears in the doorway.

There's a certain kind of man who would exploit this kind of situation, isn't there.

Mike Does he want to see the garden?

Liz I think it's too dark.

Mike I'm afraid it faces north.

James You do know that sill is rotten?

Mike No, which one is that?

38

James The one in here. I was saying to Clair: you could get your finger in there up to the knuckle. (*Laughs.*) She seemed quite confident that you would have it repaired.

Liz Well . . . (*She looks at Mike.*)

Mike Well yes, if . . .

James Well that's settled. Good.

'

Are you taking the carpets? I noticed something's been spilled on this one. What is it? Wine?

Mike Turmeric, it's turmeric.

James What's that?

Liz It's a spice, a colouring.

James Turmeric. So are you taking them?

Mike They'd be negotiable.

James Only if you are it will save me the bother you see of ripping them out.

Liz The thing is, is Clair has explained our position, hasn't she?

James That's right. She says you're prepared to ditch your buyer for a cash sale.

Mike Well not exactly ditch . . .

James No? Well then we must be at cross purposes, because she told me you would.

Liz No, yes, that's right, we probably will.

James You probably will.

Liz Well we almost certainly will, won't we Mike, only we still have qualms.

James Have I misunderstood?

Mike What Liz means is it's more a matter of how we proceed.

Liz That's right.

James But if you still have qualms . . .

Mike Yes, about how to proceed.

James Well isn't that obvious?

Mike Well not entirely . . .

James I mean if you simply instruct Clair . . .

Liz Well obviously it would be through Clair . . .

James Because I need to be clear in my own mind. You either ditch them or you don't.

Mike Right.

All faint laugh.

Well I think we will, don't you?

Liz The thing is, is the Harraps are in Shropshire.

Mike I think we'd probably feel differently, wouldn't we, if . . .

Liz And of course there's a problem with her spine.

Mike Apparently she has a crumbly spine.

James A what?

Mike A crumbly spine.

James A crumbly spine.

Led by James, all three let themselves go with hearty laughter.

James (*wiping his eyes*) So they're quite old.

Liz No, they're like us apparently.

    ,

James Listen, I like what I've seen very much.

Mike Well obviously we'll . . .

James That's right, I think the next thing I should do is speak again to Clair. I must say I think we're very lucky to be dealing with Clair. Because I have a feeling she's honest.

Mike That's right. A lot of them aren't.

James A lot of them are crooks, let's face it.

Liz I just wish she wasn't quite so cold.

Mike What? Clair?

Liz Yes. I find her cold. Cold and rather impenetrable.

Mike (*on 'impenetrable'*) I wouldn't've called her cold.

James She seems perfectly human.

Mike Well that's right. Because a lot of them aren't.

James Some of those young men . . .

    Mike and James laugh.

Liz I just think you could never get to know somebody like that.

James But is it really necessary to know people in that way? Because what you call cold, isn't that just a way of dealing with strangers. Because in a city you spend so much time dealing, don't you, with strangers. And I'm not sure what would be achieved by letting them all see into your heart. Personally I find that kind of intimacy rather stifling. No, I'd much rather feel I can walk right past someone I've known for years without the least obligation to acknowledge them. I like to know that our clothes can touch for a moment on the crowded pavement, but our eyes, even if they meet, which is unlikely, our eyes agree to say nothing. And why should we speak? (*He makes to go.*) No, I wouldn't've called her cold.

Liz So you'll talk to Clair.

James I'll talk to her in the morning.

Mike She has put you in the picture about the price.

James Yes, a hundred and ninety, is that right?

Mike Yes, as a rough guide.

James I'm sorry?

Mike Well Clair's probably told you that we're, well looking for a slightly better figure.

James No, she didn't mention that.

Mike Because . . .

Liz Because Clair feels, I think she feels we've been a bit, well cautious with the price quite frankly.

James Cautious.

Liz Yes.

James No. No she didn't tell me that.

,

Well look, I'll talk to her in the morning.

Mike (*faint laugh*) It's a hateful business, isn't it.

James I know, I know. Goodbye.

Liz Goodnight.

 Mike shows James out. The baby is crying.

Anna. (*louder*) Anna, she's awake. Anna, Gina's awake.

A moment passes. The crying stops, Mike returns.

Mike What is it?

Liz She's awake.

Mike Anna will go.

Liz Poor Anna.

Both laugh. They embrace.

What do you think?

Mike Well what do you think?

Liz Well obviously he's genuine.

Mike Yes.

Liz But he was surprised about the price.

Mike No, he was bluffing.

Liz Yes, I thought he was bluffing.

,

He deals in pictures.

Mike What, you had a chat?

Liz I actually think he's rather charming.

Mike What?

Liz Mr James.

,

Mike Is he? (*He moves away.*)

,

What sort of pictures?

Liz (*faint laugh*) I've no idea.

Blackout.

43

SCENE SIX

*Morning. Ashley in white overalls, back turned, is
examining the ceiling.*

    Anna appears in the hall doorway and stops.

    *Throughout this scene Ashley shows no sexual interest
in Anna.*

Anna Sorry.

Ashley No, it's OK. You can come through.

Anna I want to go to the kitchen.

Ashley Sure. Go ahead.

> *Anna goes out. Ashley spreads a dust-sheet. She
> returns.*

Ashley You lost?

Anna Lost?

Ashley You look lost.

Anna No. I'm not lost. I'm looking for matches. (*She
has an unlit cigarette between her fingers.*) Usually there
are matches. In the kitchen.

Ashley Italian?

Anna I'm sorry?

Ashley You Italian?

Anna Yes. Do you have a match?

Ashley (*on 'match'*) That's right you've got those eyes.
You see my wife's Italian – well half-Italian – she's got
those eyes. So whereabouts you from?

Anna Naples.

Ashley Yeah that's nice. Naples is nice. Her mother's from Turin – you know – Fiat. You know Turin at all?

Anna Yes, a little.

Ashley (*with Italian accent*) *Torino*, yeah?

Both faint laugh.

Know who's always got a match?

Anna What?

Ashley A plumber. That's what you need. For that cigarette. Is a plumber.

While Anna absorbs this, Ashley takes out a wallet and shows it to her.

Look: that's Anna.

Anna Anna.

Ashley That's right. Anna's my wife. Then that's Lisa, Timothy and Rachel. Three, eighteen months, two months. Handful, yeah.

Anna is not very interested.

No, that's alright. Have a look. (*He moves away, leaving Anna with the pictures, and spreads another sheet.*) Handful, yeah.

So, what, you studying are you.

Anna (*giving back the wallet*) I'm the nanny.

Ashley The nanny. Right.

'

So how many've they got then?

Anna One.

Ashley One.

45

Anna It's a girl.

Ashley Well then you're laughing aren't you.

Anna Sorry?

Ashley Just one, you're laughing.

,

So, what, she goes out to work does she?

Anna Mmm?

Ashley Mrs Walsum. Goes out to work.

Anna Oh no.

Ashley No.

,

Right.

Anna She's very busy though. Always.

Ashley Right.

,

Anna, my wife, she'd like to, you know, she'd like to go back to work.

Anna Yes?

Ashley (*faint laugh*) So how old is she?

Anna I don't know. She says twenty-nine, but I think at least thirty, thirty-one.

Ashley I mean the kid.

Anna The kid, she's six months.

Ashley Six months, well then she sleeps a lot, yeah? I mean I think they do, particularly girls.

Anna I think particularly boys sleep a lot.

46

Ashley Yeah? Yeah you may be right.

Anna And you know she wakes up six-thirty in the morning.

Ashley Yeah? Six-thirty, that's when I leave the house.

   Anna is about to go.

Come here come here, I want to show you something. No it's alright, I just want to show you something. Look. No no, look at this. (*He indicates the ceiling.*) Because what your governor wants me to do, alright, is hack out that sill, because he's right, it's rotten. But if I was him *that's* what would worry me. Because what you're looking at up there is a fractured cornice, and for my money it means the joists of this floor we're standing on are decaying, you with me?

   '

Because of course this is a very nice road. It's very quiet. You're near the green. There's a nice atmosphere. New cars. Trees. But I've been in one or two of these houses, and once you get the boards up . . . (*Laughs, shakes his head.*) I mean what we're talking about here is serious timber decay, we're talking about the structure, you with me?

Anna The structure.

Ashley That's right. I mean I live on a railway myself, and it's nothing special but it's what I call a proper house. The sills 've got throats. You know what I mean by a throat? A throat, it's a groove runs under the sill. It clears the water. These sills, they've got no throats. The water can't get away.

   Liz appears in the hall doorway. Anna conceals her cigarette.

47

Of course the kids love the trains. Well it's stimulation for them, isn't it.

Liz There won't be a lot of dust, will there?

Ashley Shouldn't be.

Liz It's just we have a baby.

Ashley Shouldn't be, love.

Liz Fine, that's fine. Anna, do you think you could go and get dressed now.

  Anna goes.

It's quite impossible to get that girl dressed before eleven o'clock. (*faint laugh*)

Ashley Anna?

Liz Yes, she's Italian.

Ashley Yeah, my wife's Italian.

Liz (*with indifference*) Really? Is she?

Ashley Well half-Italian. Her mother's from Turin.

Liz (*on 'mother'*) Look, I have to go out so I'd better give you this now. (*She gives him a cheque folded in half.*) Yes, look I'm sorry, I've only just realised I don't have the cash. You don't mind a cheque, do you.

  ,

Because obviously you'd rather have the cash obviously, but somehow this morning things have . . . Well I'm sure you must have mornings like that.

Ashley It's just that we did say . . .

Liz Look, I know. Well if you'd rather wait.

  ,

48

Ashley No no. It's fine.

Liz Because look, if you're prepared to wait.

Ashley It's not a problem.

Liz Look, I feel awful about this.

Ashley No. Please. It's not a problem.

Liz It is right, isn't it. (*i.e. the amount*)

Ashley Sure it is, yeah. (*He pockets the cheque without looking at it.*)

Liz Well if there's any problem.

,

Ashley Right.

Liz makes to go, turns back.

Liz Will there be a lot of noise?

Ashley Shouldn't be.

Liz Only she's asleep.

Ashley Well if you could find me something . . .

Liz How's that? Well of course, yes, what is it?

Ashley I mean if you could find me something like a blanket I could wrap it round my hammer.

Liz forces a smile.
Blackout.

SCENE SEVEN

Morning.
  James and Clair.

James (*with enthusiasm*) It's beginning to feel like home, isn't it. Don't you think that's a good sign?

Clair Mr Walsum's had the sill repaired.

James I know he has. Wasn't that prompt of him. Can I get you lunch?

Clair I'm sorry?

James I wondered if after this you would like lunch somewhere.

Clair I've got sandwiches.

James Sandwiches.

Clair Yes, I've got sandwiches in the office.

      ,

James Well, another time.

Clair The Walsums are very pleased with your offer.

James Well naturally I'm very pleased they've accepted. Because it's important who you buy from and I think they're rather nice people, don't you, Clair?

  Clair smiles.

No, you're quite right, they're not at all are they. Not like us for example. Because we *are*, aren't we, we *are* nice people. Well aren't we nice people?

  Clair smiles.

No you're quite right, we're not at all.

Clair Speak for yourself.

James What? (*brief laugh*)

'

Look, I'm sorry to have dragged you back.

Clair Yes, I wasn't quite clear –

James I just want to be sure.

'

Two hundred thousand pounds. (*confidentially*) Do you think it's worth it Clair? Am I being made a fool of?

Clair I'm not buying it.

James Yes, but do you?

Clair Yes I do.

James Well I'm glad you said that, Clair. Because so do I. And after all, what's money?

Clair smiles.

Well. Yes.

'

Clair This road will always be desirable.

James Listen: a train stops right outside your window. The passengers' faces are all pressed against the glass. Doesn't that worry you?

Clair You get used to trains. You don't think about them.

James What are they anyway, are they egg? Your sandwiches. Are they egg?

Clair No.

51

James I'll tell you something. And of course I may be completely wrong. But I'm pretty certain you have one of those beds, don't you, that folds up into a sofa. Is that right? Look, I'm sorry, I'm not embarrassing you, am I? All I mean is, is it begins as a sofa. You spend the evening sitting on it, most probably on your own. Then at a certain time, and although the time is utterly up to you, it's probably always the same time near enough, you get off the sofa, and you unfold it and rearrange it in a special way which once seemed rather complicated but now comes to you as second nature, and you get ready for bed and you get into it. Please stop me if I'm wrong. And in the morning you are woken by the alarm – if not by the trains – and you get up, and you get ready for work. But before you go out, you turn the bed back into a sofa again. Except on those days – and this is the nub – except for those days when you're late for work perhaps, or you simply can't face it, you simply can't face folding the bloody thing up. So you leave it. But the moment you get home in the evening you take one look at it, you take one look at it and you regret having left it like that. Unmade like that. Bitterly. Because immediately there is a dilemma. I don't think it's too much to speak of a dilemma, do you. And the last thing any of us wants is a dilemma, particularly in the evenings. Because either you turn your bed back into a sofa, knowing that in a few hours you'll have to turn your sofa back into a bed again. Or of course you leave it. The disadvantage in this case being that desolate feeling that nothing in the room has really happened to distinguish between morning, evening, and night.

Clair (*not unamused*) No, I'm afraid you're completely wrong.

James Because there are times when I think it must be rather terrible to live on your own.

Clair What makes you think I live on my own?

,

I like being on my own.

James It has its advantages.

Clair It certainly does.

Both faint laugh.

Your wife hasn't been, has she.

James She trusts my judgement.

Clair Isn't she curious?

James I'll let you into a secret: I've decided not to tell her till we exchange. A house in London, she's absolutely no idea.

Clair The thing is is Mr and Mrs Walsum want to exchange within the next couple of weeks if possible.

James Yes, of course.

Clair Because they did already have a firm offer.

James Which they rejected.

Clair Yes, but on the understanding there'd be a speedy exchange of contracts.

James Yes.

,

Listen –

Clair I think they'd feel happier if they'd heard from your solicitors.

James I'm instructing them this afternoon.

Clair Fine, that's fine. It's simply that –

James Then I'm afraid I'm going on to Rome. A client of mine wants me to take a look at a picture. It's a complete waste of time. You can see from the slides it's not genuine. For one thing it appears to have more than one vanishing point which is a curiosity to say the least for the period in question.

Clair Right, so what exactly is your position now?

James You know what I mean by vanishing point?

,

Listen, you seem to be asking me whether I'm honest.

Clair Well of course not, it's simply that –

James Because quite frankly Clair –

Clair I'm sorry, it's simply that they were beginning to panic.

James Well please set their minds at rest.

Clair And I think they feel that since they've deferred to you –

James In what way have they deferred to me?

Clair In that they did have a firm offer.

James Which they rejected.

Clair Yes, but since they've now deferred –

James I think you'll find that I have deferred to them, Clair, in this business.

Brief sound of laughter off.

Is there somebody here?

They listen. Silence. Clair moves to the hall doorway.

Clair (*calls*) Hello? (*louder*) Hello?

54

Silence.

There shouldn't be. (*She fiddles with the keys.*)

James Perhaps it's next door. Those are flats next door, aren't they.

Clair Yes, but they're owner-occupied.

James Like yours.

Clair (*laughs*) I couldn't afford to live here.

James But the principle is the same. They all have beds that fold into chairs. These . . . Harraps, they're eating their hearts out, are they.

Clair They've been a little aggressive on the phone.

James Have they? I love it up there by the Welsh border, don't you. If only it wasn't death. Because it's very beautiful, but really it is death.

Clair So we're talking about maybe a fortnight.

James At the outside, Clair.

Clair Well I'll tell them.

James Not egg.

,

Do you know Italy at all?

Clair I've been to Venice.

James Seven days was that, or a long weekend?

Clair I'm sorry, I don't like being laughed at.

James Laughed at? Clair . . .

,

Unfortunately I have to fly. Because my real passion is for trains, particularly sleeping trains. I think a cubicle in a train is perhaps the most perfect place to sleep, don't you. There's hot water and prohibitions in several languages. The rhythm of the track lulls you asleep. You dream your way under the mountains, then when you wake up, you lift the blind and the Mediterranean is right outside the window, lapping on empty beaches. In the east the sun's coming up behind the vineyards, and the great marble cities: Pisa, Florence, Rome, Naples.

'

For some people sleeping on trains is a kind of compulsion, did you know that? Last thing at night they disappear from the end of the platform. They jump down onto the ballast and follow the electrified rails until they find an unlocked train. Of course the water in the first-class washrooms has gone cold, but the benches retain some warmth at least from the last passengers. Yes I know it might be argued they have no other homes, but I think the truth of it is, deep in their hearts, they're in love with trains, don't you.

'

All I meant Clair, was that personally twenty-four hours in Venice is too much for me. What a foul wet place. Thank god it's sinking.

Blackout.

Act Two

SCENE ONE

Night. Anna kneels downstage with cards, playing patience on the floor, beside her a glass of orange juice. Mike and Liz are sprawled on a sofa, drinking wine. Mike is noticeably drunk.

Mike I just mean, look all I mean is, well come on, I'm right.

Liz I don't think you are. I'm sorry.

Mike Well come on, you know I'm right. Because look, you're in a room, right, with a man –

Liz (*with a laugh*) I'm sorry, you don't know. You just don't know what you're talking about.

Mike No come on, come on. Listen to me. You're not listening to me. I mean you know what I'm talking about, don't you, Anna? (*Anna takes no notice. Mike faint laugh*) Yeah, that's right. You see Anna will bear me out on this. Because you're in a room right, with a man. Or anywhere, not just a room, anywhere. And there you are. There you are and you're talking about, well look I'm not talking about what you're talking about, because that's not my point – I mean come on come on if you won't listen . . . Because the point is, and look this is my point, is you both know, you *both know* what's going on. But no one admits it, that's all. I mean you can say what you like –

Liz I didn't say a word.

Mike Yeah, say what you like but you know – you *both*

57

know – that I'm right because this – listen I don't see that it's funny – because this is human nature.

Liz It's certainly your nature.

Mike Alright, well that's what I'm saying. (*He points at Anna's cards.*) Snap. (*faint laugh. Anna looks up briefly.*) I didn't know Italians played that.

Liz Patience?

Mike Yeah yeah. Patience.

  '

What did I say? I mean take, let's take Clair for example.

Liz (*laughs*) Clair?

Mike Yeah yeah. I mean what's so funny, I mean that's just an example isn't it. Clair. The waitress. Because, what, you know, I've spoken to Clair, what, a few times, quite a few times now, and that's exactly the sort of thing I mean. Because, you know, it's prices . . . it's properties . . . it's a serious business, but we both know what's going on, Clair and me, because that's what's always going on. And d'you see, that's all I'm saying. (*Mike leans forward to pour wine into Anna's glass. She puts her hand over it without looking up.*) That's all I mean. Look at this, she's Italian, she doesn't drink.

Liz You mean you want to rape Clair.

Mike No no no. Come on. Come *on*, will you. Because who's talking about violence? (*to Anna*) Did I say anything about violence? No I mean what is this? I mean I'm just talking about something that happens, something you know that happens, and here you are, here the two of you are, and you're trying to turn it into a moral issue.

Liz (*amused*) Who said anything about a moral issue?

Mike Because what you're both trying to do is completely distort what I'm trying to say. Because – no it's not, it's not funny – because I'm not talking about violence, aggression, or whatever. Because alright, we know there's something going on, and it's sexual, but it's based on respect. Respect is all part of it. I mean what does she mean, what do you mean rape Clair. Because let's face it we're not talking about, I don't know . . . Arabs, are we. We're not talking about, you know, Italians, are we Anna, or anything like that. I mean I'm not criticising but it's different, that's a different kind of society.

Anna I'm going to bed.

Liz Goodnight.

Anna goes.

Mike Yeah, goodnight. (*Calls after Anna.*) Look, no offence. (*faint laugh*)

Mike drinks.

Liz You know she's been phoning Italy again.

Mike Mmm?

Liz Anna. I caught her on the phone again to Italy.

Mike How d'you know?

Liz Because she was speaking Italian. (*She drinks.*) Although of course she denied it.

Mike She denied she was speaking Italian.

Liz She denied it was Italy.

'

Mike Sometimes there's no one there, you know. The whole of Italy. No one there. Turin. Pisa. Florence. Rome. Naples . . .

Liz (*on 'Rome'*) I mean why can't she *write* to her mother?

Mike The lights are all on but there's nobody there.

'

Look, she knows the position on phone calls.

Liz lies with her head on Mike's lap.

Liz Anyway she'd eat you alive.

Mike What?

Liz Clair.

Mike Well *I* wouldn't mind.

Both faint laugh.

Liz Let's go to bed.

Mike Because what's he coming back for anyway?

Liz He wants to measure up.

Mike Measure up. What does he want to measure up?

Liz I don't know.

Mike Because what did he do last time?

Liz Well obviously not measure up.

Both find this funny.

Mike So this is what Clair said.

Liz Clair was at lunch.

Mike They let them out, do they, for lunch. Because he does know I suppose, he does know in two days we exchange.

Liz Well of course he does.

Mike Well as long as he knows.

Liz Well of course he does. Let's go to bed.

Mike (*amused*) You know he's never been outside, don't you.

Liz (*amused*) What?

Mike Clair told me –

Liz In one of your conversations.

Mike In one of our conversations she said to me, he's never been out in the garden.

Liz So?

Mike Well you'd think he'd be curious.

Liz Well obviously he isn't.

Both find this funny.

Mike Because I think he's cold.

Liz Well I think he's charming.

Mike Anyway, you can ask him.

Liz Ask him if he's charming?

Mike If he's curious. No, you can ask him tomorrow if he's curious at all.

Liz I won't be here tomorrow. I've told you: I'm at the flat.

'

Mike You're at the flat. Right. So how's the flat?

Liz The flat is fine. It's just –

Mike Look, if we don't take this flat we won't be cash.

Liz I know, I know.

Mike Because if you want people to treat you like . . .

Liz I know.

Mike Shit. Or whatever. Eating your heart out. Or whatever.

,

What're you looking at?

Liz What's that line?

Mike It's a crack. Just a crack.

Liz It's just I think, you know, we might begin to get on top of each other.

Mike Well I'm sure we might. I'm sure that's, you know, a strong possibility. (*They laugh.*) Or whatever.

,

Liz Come on, let's go upstairs.

Mike What's wrong?

Liz Anna might come in.

Mike Anna might come in. (*faint laugh*) You're right.

Liz Well she might.

Mike Yes she might. I'm sure that's, you know, a strong possibility.

Liz Come on. (*She gets up.*)

Mike I mean she knows what I'm talking about. Anna knows what I mean, don't you Anna.

Liz takes her glass and reaches for the bottle to clear it away.

Hey.

Mike stops her and drains the bottle into his glass. Liz then takes her own glass and the empty bottle out into the kitchen. Mike stretches out, but doesn't drink, leaving his glass on the floor.

Because there you are, I mean, you both know – you *both know* – what's going on . . . Because, well that's all we're talking about isn't it . . . (*faint laugh. Then, after a moment, a longer louder laugh as if something unexpectedly amusing has struck him.*)

Liz reappears at the doorway.

Liz Are you coming? (*She goes up to him. Gently*) Come on, let's go to bed.

She touches him. He's asleep. Liz remains a moment, then goes.
Blackout.

SCENE TWO

Morning. The cards from the previous night remain on the floor where Anna left them. Clair and James enter.

James (*laughs*) But I'd love to see it.

Clair (*laughs*) I don't think you would.

James And what colour are the walls?

Clair The walls?

James Yes.

Clair *I* don't know. Neutral.

James Neutral? (*laughs*)

Clair Absolutely neutral. (*Laughs.*) They don't take sides.

63

James Clair. A joke!

Clair Yes.

James Well I'm amazed. I'm amazed and amused. And you?

Clair And me what?

James Do *you* take sides?

Clair I don't understand.

James Or are you just neutral. Like the wall.

Clair Oh, I'm like the wall. That's my job.

James Impenetrable.

Clair If you like.

James And there's a shelf.

Clair A what?

James On the wall. The bathroom wall. A little glass shelf and a tube of toothpaste that lasts for months and months and months.

Clair Really?

James I'm sorry. I'm prying.

Clair You're good at that.

James Yes I am, aren't I.

Both laugh. Then silence.

When I rang do you know they wanted to send somebody else. They were trying to fob me off with one of those dreadful boys.

Clair Toby.

James You're right. That was the name. He said, I'll come and meet you with the key. I said will you please listen to me, I'm dealing exclusively with Clair in this matter.

  Both laugh.

What's he like?

Clair Toby? (*Shrugs.*)

James Would we 've hit it off?

Clair No.

  They laugh.

James Is he in front of you or behind you?

Clair He's to the side.

James The left.

Clair Yes.

James You turn to your left and there's Toby. He's on the phone but he's looking at you.

Clair No, he's working.

  ,

James Yes, of course he is.

Clair I asked him to come.

James Did you?

Clair I should be at lunch.

James We can have lunch after this.

Clair Because now we're having to work in the evenings . . .

James And this is work.

Clair Yes. Yes, it's a long day.

,

James Yes, of course it is.

Clair Sometimes it's a strain dealing with people.

James I can imagine.

Clair Because we're caught in the middle of it.

James Which is what you're paid for.

Clair Yes.

James Whatever per cent. And you enjoy it.

Clair Yes.

James Because you like dealing with people. You like people.

Clair Yes. Yes I do.

James So why is it you don't seem happy, Clair?

Clair I'm perfectly happy.

James But you don't sound happy.

Clair (*with anger*) Well I'm sorry.

,

James Listen, I ought to get on. (*He takes out a folding surveyor's rule.*) It will be rather unfortunate if these pieces of mine don't fit.

James measures. Clair, still angry, moves away and pokes at the cards with her shoe.

Clair I'm sorry if I don't 'sound happy'. You'll have to tell me what 'happy' sounds like.

66

James measures, says nothing. Clair laughs in spite of herself.

And it's not a bathroom. It's a shower-room. If we don't describe things accurately, there can be misunderstandings.

James (*without looking up*) I'm sure.

Clair And we try to avoid – obviously – avoid – misunderstandings. We try not to give people expectations that can't be fulfilled. Or they feel cheated. Disappointed. And of course they *blame* us.

James (*as before*) For what?

Clair (*shrugs*) For everything. (*Smiles.*) But yes, there is a little glass shelf. How did you know that?

James (*looks up at her*) Oh, there's always a little glass shelf, Clair. Just above the sink.

Both faint laugh.

Do you know what turmeric is?

Clair You put it in curry. It makes it yellow.

James That's right.
I'll need to come along there.

Clair kneels and begins picking up the cards.

Clair How was Rome?

James How was Rome?

,

Look, you shouldn't be doing that. Hot. Rome was hot.

Clair And you exchange tomorrow.

James Tomorrow morning.

Clair finishes clearing up the cards. James stops measuring and watches. She senses his look and turns.

You shouldn't've done that.

Clair moves out of the way. He measures.

Clair Your wife must be excited.

James Must she?

Clair I thought you said you'd told her.

James Yes I did. Yes I have. And yes you're right she *is*. And of course the boy. Because it's a miserable life for Mark in that hotel. (*Clair looks at him.*) It's not good for a boy, is it. Do you have children?

Clair No.

James I've asked you that before. And you gave me the same answer. You have no children. You live on your own. You're very happy on your own. I'm sorry. Because I think it's a kind of measure, isn't it, of people. There's a way of measuring people by listening to how often they repeat themselves. With some it's just the same thing every day. But with others – drunks for example, the insane – it's the same every moment of every day. And here am I repeating myself. Because it's funny isn't it, how you are terribly aware of everybody else's faults, and then you find you share them too.

Clair (*with a laugh*) Speak for yourself.

James also laughs. He folds up the rule.

Well?

James What's that?

Clair Will they fit?

James Do you know I'm hopeless at this sort of thing. What do *you* think?

Both laugh.

Clair Look, really we ought to go.

James But you're at lunch.

Clair is holding the cards, flicking through them with her thumb.

James Do you know, I think we're going to be very happy here. Since this will be our smallest house, but our biggest city. And I think there's a lot of nonsense spoken about cities, don't you. Because yes yes yes, we all know that strangers live next door to strangers. We've all passed friends in the street because the moment of recognition has occurred too late, and you're both too embarrassed – or something else – too . . . fixed, too fixed in your mind to turn. And yes yes yes, we've all, as strangers, woken up in the morning to find our faces inches away from the open eyes of another stranger. We get up. We dress on opposite sides of the bed. Then we fold the bed away maybe . . . A little ashamed perhaps, or at any rate too preoccupied to speak. But what does any of that matter? Because surely the great advantage is, that since we don't know each other, since we've never seen into each other's hearts, then we respect each other.

Clair That would be nice if it was true.

James Isn't it true?

Clair faint laugh.

And have you described this accurately?

Clair This what?

James May I have those? (*He takes the cards from Clair.*) This what? This . . . situation. (*He cuts the cards.*)

Clair I hope so. Yes.

James (*giving her half the cards*) Beggar my neighbour. What do you say.

Clair (*laughs*) Please . . .

James Well what then?

Clair Look, I don't play cards.

James You don't play cards? Is this a matter of principle with you?

Clair (*laughs*) No . . .

James So what about snap then? You're not going to make a moral issue out of snap, are you. Money's not involved after all. Only chance. (*He sits.*) Yes yes yes, you have to go. Listen, one or two minutes, that's all.

A moment passes. Clair sits to play.

Well there you are.

Clair I should be at lunch.

James Well you are at lunch. This *is* lunch. Please.

Clair lays the first card. Laying of cards gradually accelerates.

James (*with loud enthusiasm*) Snap!

He takes his cards. They lay cards as before.

Snap!

He takes his cards. They lay cards as before until James indicates to Clair to stop.

Well?

Clair faint laugh.

James These two cards, aren't they the same?

Clair Yes.

James Well.

,

You don't seem to be entering into the spirit.

,

Look, I'm giving you a chance, Clair. I wouldn't give everybody this kind of chance.

Clair faint laugh.

Well? What is it you have to say?

Clair Look, I . . . (*She gets up.*)

James Please, you have to say it.

Clair I'm sorry, but this is ridiculous.

James (*on 'ridiculous'*) No it's not ridiculous. I've said it. You must say it.

,

Clair Snap.

James What?

Clair Snap.

James (*loud*) What? Snap?

Clair Yes.

James Yes, well say it.

Clair (*loud*) SNAP. (*Laughs.*)

James (*gets up and gives her the cards*) These are yours.
No. All of them. Please. They're all yours. You've won.

She takes the cards.

Clair We ought to go.

James So what are you doing about eating?

Clair I've got sandwiches.

James Well, another time.

Clair Yes.

James What? (*loud*) What?

Clair (*loud*) YES.

Both laugh.

James Good.

,

But we won't will we.

Clair I shouldn't think so.

James No. I shouldn't think so either.

Sound of laughter off.

Is there somebody here?

They listen. Silence. Clair moves to the hall doorway.

Clair (*calls*) Hello? (*louder*) Hello?

Silence.

There shouldn't be. (*She comes back to James.*)

James It strikes me we're rather similar people, aren't
we? I mean what is it, is there something wrong with us
perhaps, that's what I'm beginning to wonder. Because

here we are, we've been together in this room, this house, twice now. And –

Clair Three times.

,

James Is it?

,

Do you know what I'd very much like to do now, Clair.

Clair is about to speak but breaks off as she notices James's gaze shift to a point behind her. She turns to see Anna standing in the hall doorway.

Clair Oh. Hello. I'm sorry about this.

Anna It's my day off.

Clair Yes, I'm sorry. I was told there'd be no one here.

Anna This is my day off.

Clair Yes of course. (*to James*) They told me the house would be empty.

Vittorio, a young man smoking a cigarette, comes in behind Anna and puts his arms around her waist. She puts her hands on his.

Anyway. Listen. I think we've – haven't we – finished – is that right?

Anna Please don't tell Mrs Walsum.

Clair (*to James*) You didn't want to look upstairs. Did you?

Vittorio (*sotto voce*) Non è la loro, vero?

Anna (*sotto voce*) No, lei è l'agente immobiliare.

Vittorio Cosa? Ha la chiave?

Anna Non ha importanza.

Anna takes the cigarette and inhales before returning it to Vittorio's hand. Neither of them shows any embarrassment.

Clair Listen, I'm sorry if we've . . . Look, I was told there'd be no one here.

Anna Please don't tell them, OK.

Vittorio Guarderanno di sopra?

Anna No. Se ne andranno.

Vittorio Ma tu passerai dei guai.

Anna No. Non lo diranno a nessuno.

James Well of course we won't. Of course we won't tell anyone.

Anna Thank you.

Vittorio and Anna go.

James Do you know what I'd very much like to do now, Clair. I'd like to go out into the garden.

Blackout.

SCENE THREE

Afternoon. Liz and Mike. Both quiet and tense.

Mike Well he might show. I suppose he might still show.

Liz Yes.

Mike I mean what are they doing, are they phoning?

Liz They've been phoning.

Mike Well are they sending someone?

Liz I don't know.

Mike Well you've spoken to them.

Liz I told you I don't know.

,

Mike I'm sorry.

,

Liz I mean –

Mike (*overlapping*) But listen –

,

Well come on.

Liz Nothing.

Mike You were going to say something.

Liz It's nothing.

,

All I was going to say was –

Mike I mean since you interrupted me.

Liz Well go on then.

Mike No no. Please. You were going to say something.

,

Liz All I was going to say was, is, it's obvious he's not going to.

Mike Is that what they said?

Liz No, but it's obvious.

Mike I don't see that it's obvious.

Liz You know it's obvious.

,

Look, we both know it's obvious.

Mike But he must have a number, he must have an address.

Liz Yes.

Mike Well are they sending someone?

Liz Well obviously not.

Mike Is that what they said?

Liz Look, I can't repeat . . .

Mike I know you can't.

Liz . . . word for word what they said.

Mike I know you can't, but they must've said something.

Liz I've told you what they said.

Mike Well it keeps changing.

Liz It doesn't keep changing. They appreciate our position but there's nothing they can do.

Mike Well I'm sorry but I find that hard to believe.

Liz Well you speak to them.

Mike I'm not speaking to them.

,

I'm not speaking to them: all I want to know is to know what's happening.

Liz We know what's happened.

Mike We don't know what's happened. What's happened is everyone thinks they know what's happened.

Liz Well it's obvious what's happened.

Mike Well I don't see that it's obvious.

'

Well I'm sorry, and perhaps there's something wrong with me but I don't see that it's at all obvious, because the fact remains –

Liz Well look, if you refuse to see it –

Mike The fact remains that what we're talking about here are two quite unrelated things.

Liz Well of course they're related.

Mike Yes, that's the assumption.

Liz Well if you refuse to be realistic about it –

Mike I'm sorry, I'm sorry, but look what is this? What is this? Because what I'm trying to be *is* realistic, that's exactly my point. Because everyone else is just letting their imagination –

Liz (*on 'imagination'*) Well listen, you talk to them.

Mike I'm not talking to them.

Liz Well if you won't talk to them.

'

Mike Because the fact remains –

Liz I mean if you won't even talk to them.

Mike The fact remains, doesn't it, that we know her movements and we know she went back to work in the afternoon.

Liz No.

,

No she didn't.

Mike You said she did.

Liz I've already told you she didn't.

Mike You said she didn't go in this morning.

Liz I said – if you'd listened you would've heard that what I said was was she hasn't been in this morning and she didn't go back yesterday afternoon.

Mike Well if you'd told me that.

Liz I have told you that.

Mike I mean if you'd just told me that in the first place.

,

It's all we need, isn't it.

Liz Mike.

Mike I just mean this is all we need.

Liz Yes but there is Clair, there is Clair to consider.

Mike Well fuck quite frankly, fuck Clair.
    No, look, I'm sorry, I'm sorry. Because if that's what's happened although I still don't really see that it's likely then naturally, naturally I have every sympathy for Clair. But Jesus Christ the fact remains the man was supposed to exchange. Because couldn't he 've waited? Yes yes yes I know it's terrible.

,

I mean obviously . . .

,

78

Fuck.

        ,

Look, you know I like Clair. I've always said: I like Clair.

Liz Yes I know.

Mike Well what's that supposed to mean?

        ,

I mean what is that supposed to mean exactly?

Liz I just mean if you'd gone round with him instead . . .

Mike That's Clair's job. Clair is paid – she is paid – by us – whatever per cent – to go round with people. Because –

Liz Alright. I know.

Mike Well come on.

        ,

I mean if she can't look after herself.

        ,

Because listen, let's be realistic about this. What are we supposed to imagine? Are we supposed to imagine he took her by the throat and dragged her off . . .

Liz No obviously not.

Mike Dragged her off in broad daylight – this was what, lunchtime – to his . . . whatever it was.

        ,

Liz BMW.

Mike BMW.

   Both faint laugh. They relax a little.

Because –

Liz No, obviously it wasn't like that.

Mike Well then.

'

And you say Anna was here.

Liz That's right.

Mike And she witnessed this . . . I don't know . . . rape, abduction, or whatever.

Liz (*on 'rape'*) Well obviously it's more complicated than that.

Mike Because isn't it rather condescending to assume that Clair is a victim in this? Because given the choice, who's to say she'd not rather go somewhere, do something, go somewhere interesting, rather than trot off back to work and sell houses.

Liz The French Pyrenees.

Mike What?

'

Liz Look, let's not argue about it.

Mike So what was Anna doing here anyway?

Liz I've no idea.

Mike Well surely you asked.

Liz I haven't had time.

Mike But you've spoken to her. Because she was meant to be out all day.

Liz Yes I know she was.

Mike So what was she doing in the house?

Liz Well how do I know what she was doing in the house?

Mike We ought to talk to her.

Liz Well you talk to her.

Mike I'm not talking to her.

The baby is crying.

Fuck.

Liz Mmm?

Mike She's awake.

,

Anyway, what did they have to say?

Liz Well, they were apologetic.

Mike You mentioned the Harraps. (*i.e. to the agent*)

Liz No, we've lost the Harraps.

Mike You're sure.

Liz They're building a complex. They've got permission to build one of these . . . a timeshare complex on the land.

Mike But it's protected.

Liz Obviously not.

Mike So they're laughing.

The crying has grown louder.

Jesus Christ.

Liz (*goes to doorway*) Anna. (*louder*) Anna.
The thing was (*faint laugh*) well I don't know but I felt he was implying –

Mike Which one is that?

Liz It was Toby.

Mike What, at the back?

Liz No, he's on the right as you go in. No, I felt that he –

Mike Toby.

Liz Yes, was implying that we could, well I'm fairly sure this is what he was trying to say . . .

Mike Wait a moment. (*Goes to doorway and calls.*) Anna. She's awake. (*He's about to go out when the crying stops.*)

   Silence.

How d'you mean?

Liz Well I just felt he had an idea we could, well exploit the situation.

Mike Exploit it.

Liz I think so.

Mike Well is that what he said?

Liz No it's not what he *said*.

   '

All I mean is is he was talking about perhaps – because of course I agreed they should leave it on – so he just felt that perhaps it could be a good opportunity to . . . reconsider I suppose.

Mike What, the price?

Liz The price, because apparently there's been a lot of . . . activity over the past few weeks, and I think he was implying that Clair, well, had perhaps been a little too cautious.

   '

He felt for example she hadn't been making enough of the fourth bedroom.

,

Mike Well this is assuming we've lost James.

,

Liz Well I think we have to assume we've lost James.

,

Mike So he thinks two hundred is cautious.

,

Liz That's basically what he's saying.

Mike Well of course that's what we've always said ourselves.

Liz Well that's right.

Mike moves away, laughs briefly, reflects.

I mean this was all very informal because I don't want to give the wrong impression, because actually he was very upset about Clair.

Liz comes up behind Mike and puts her arms around his waist. He puts his hands on hers.

Mike What is it?

Liz Aren't you curious?

,

It's just they've been here, haven't they. They were in this house. They were in this room, that's all.

,

I mean aren't you curious?

Mike Mmm?

Liz Because in some ways I can't imagine it at all, I can't imagine where they'd begin.

'

But then I suppose they're rather similar people.

Mike D'you think?

'

Liz No, don't let go. Don't let go of me.

'

Mike Anna might come in.

Liz Well let her come in.

Blackout.

SCENE FOUR

Darkness. The sound of a high-speed train approaching. As it reaches maximum, the light comes up to reveal James talking on the phone in Clair's flat at night.

James . . . well of *course* you do. That's quite understandable. But there comes a point doesn't there where you have to let go, you just have to let go. You just have to say to yourself: *that's* her life, *that's* her choice.

Absolutely.

Well absolutely, and I do think there's a lot of nonsense spoken about cities. 'The fear.' 'The loneliness'. (*Laughs.*) Because quite frankly too much intimacy can be just as stifling. In fact you're far more likely in my experience to be stifled by a friend than by a complete stranger.

Oh yes, oh yes, there are *statistics* about it.

Well it's natural for you to worry and I'd probably do exactly the same thing in your shoes (*confidential*) because to tell you the truth I'm a bit of a worrier myself. Not the big things, oddly enough. No. It's the little things. It's the details, isn't it. It's the filling in the sandwich isn't it, or the leaf suddenly falling.

I said the leaf: the leaf suddenly falling.

Sound of train approaching.

Of course. Of course. Let me put her on.
(*Calls.*) Clair? Clair?
Just one moment and I'll put her on. (*Calls.*) Clair?

Train passes.

(*Calls loudly over train.*) Clair?

Train recedes.

She's not answering me. She must still

That's right, she's not. She must still, d'you know she must still be – can you believe it – must still be in that shower. (*Laughs with Mum.*) Yes, but the fact is they do feel soiled. Clair and her colleagues – those boys of hers – they do feel soiled after a day of buying and selling, selling and buying. They feel a kind of . . . filth, quite frankly. They feel a kind of – oh yes, hasn't she told you? – a kind of disgust with themselves.

Well of *course* she hides it from you, of *course* she does. But I happen to know that all day long, this is the moment, the one moment she dreams of: the hot water streaming and the steam, the hot steam rising.

Faint train passes.

These trains are a nuisance, aren't they.

Yes. They're almost in the room. And it's hardly a room is it – more a kind of – well that's right: more a

kind of a cupboard. When I first saw it I thought she
was dragging me screaming into a kind of large
cupboard. I said: Clair, Clair, Clair, is this where you
live? (*Laughs with Mum.*) I did. I did. I said: is this
where you live, Clair? In an over-large cupboard, Clair?
Smelling of smoke? In this odd little hole with a bed
that doesn't even fold away. Shower-room to the left.
Kitchenette to the right. Is this your . . . 'investment'?

Absolutely. But she educated me. D'you know, she
educated me. And as time's gone by, I've come to realise

Sound of train approaching.

Oh yes, *old* friends, old old friends, and I've come to
realise that this is, as it were, her sanctuary. Yes. That
there's a very good atmosphere here. That it's very calm
and quiet. That even the trains contribute to the quiet by
way, as it were, of contrast and she's taught me to see
the quiet beauty of the tracks as they converge on the
vanishing *what*?

Certainly I'll try her again. One moment. (*Calls.*)
Clair? Clair?

Train passes.

She's just rubbing herself.

I said: apparently she's just rubbing herself dry and
then she'll be out, then she'll be free. She'll be clean and
she'll be free and *what*?

I *said*: once she's thoroughly

Yes: once she's thoroughly rubbed

Please. Please. If I could finish: once she's thoroughly
rubbed herself she will, as I said, be clean and free and
the two of us will be going out just to clear up any
misunderstandings for an egg sandwich probably since
I have to be in Rome in the morning although you can
see from the slides that it's not *what*?

Faint train passes.

Well surely you're not asking me to barge in there, are you? Just barge in there, sweep everything off the little glass shelf, all the bottles and jars, all the creams and scents piled up on the little glass shelf and the torn-off bits of cotton-wool, just sweep them away and what? *demand*? – surely not *demand* that she comes to the phone? Because I don't see it's my place to demand anything of the poor child, of the poor girl which is one of those dreadful words, isn't it, one of those dreadful words men use to belittle women, I *do* apologise, I sometimes think we need, don't we need, I suspect we need to look much more deeply, don't we, into ourselves and don't misunderstand me, I don't mean this terrible thing of self, of self, of self-examination, I just mean simply a look, simply a glance to see if there's anything there at all quite frankly (*laughs*) not that I really care one way or the other *what*?

I *beg* your pardon?

You're going to put down the phone unless you can speak to your daughter? I'm *sorry*? Because how will you speak to her if you put down the phone *what*?

I thought I'd explained all that. I thought I'd made my position very clear but if you have any doubts, any lingering doubts, then you should speak to Clair because look. (*change of tone*) Look. Look, here she is now.

He turns and smiles as if someone has entered the room and focuses on this point with extreme stillness. The sound of a train approaching.

Yes, here she is now.
Look at her.
She's clean.
She's dry.
She's . . . radiant.

*With a sudden gesture he holds the receiver out at
arm's length to the imagined Clair and remains rigid
in this position to the end of the scene. Crescendo of
approaching train.*

She's patting her hair with a towel.
She wants to speak to you.

*At the moment of the train's maximum impact,
blackout. The rush and whine of the train continues –
extremely loud – fading away as the light comes up on
the final scene.*

SCENE FIVE

*Mike and Liz's garden. October evening sunlight. Mike,
Liz and Toby.*
    *Mike and Liz are drinking wine. As the lights come
up, the three of them are laughing.*
    Anna sits by the vine, reading a book.

Mike You're joking.

Toby I am not. I swear to you those were her exact
words.

Mike Consider an offer . . .

Toby That's right. 'I'm prepared to consider an offer.'

Liz But you must've *died.*

Toby And the thing is, is there she is – I mean it
wouldn't've been so bad – but there she is standing at
the top of the stairs, and all she's got on – well as far as
I could tell (*laughs*) – all she's wearing is this, well a kind
of Chinese dressing-gown, one of these . . . kimonos.

Mike Japanese, in that case.

Toby Well whatever it was I couldn't get out of there fast enough.

They all three laugh a little more. Silence.

Mike Yes, Anna's got one of those, hasn't she.

Liz One of what?

Mike One of those – whatever it is – kimonos.

Liz Has she?

Mike You know she has.

,

It's got birds on it.

Toby It's certainly very pleasant out here.

Toby Well it's quiet at least.

Mike The thing is we're not really gardeners.

Toby Well you wouldn't believe it.

Liz Because of course we used to get a lot of noise from next door, when it was flats.

Mike Well of course it still is flats.

Liz But when it was tenants.

Toby nods in sympathy.

Mike Mind you, when you think about it, there's absolutely no reason why a tenant – is there – should make any more noise than an owner-occupier.

Toby No, but I'm afraid – let's face it – I'm afraid you're talking about a completely different sort of person, a completely different sort of attitude to the property.

Liz Of course it's quite disgusting what they did to the tenants.

Mike Well it's unforgivable.

,

Liz The nice thing is, by this time of day the light's come round.

Toby glances at his watch.

Look, I'm sorry, can we get you a glass of wine?

Toby I'd rather not, actually.

Mike No no. Fine. We understand. Because obviously you must still feel – well of course it's not as if we don't still feel –

Liz Yes, but life has to go on, Mike.

Mike Well of course life has to go on. By definition life has to go on. It's just –

Toby Please. It's just a little early for me, that's all. (*faint laugh*) But I wouldn't say no to something soft.

Liz What, squash?

Toby Fine. Yes. Squash.

Mike Or a Coke or something?

Toby Squash would be fine.

Liz Anna, could you be a darling and get a glass of squash for Mr . . .

Toby Toby. Please, it's Toby.

Liz Right. Yes, of course. Could you get him a glass of orange squash.

Anna Orange squash.

Toby Or lemon. Lemon would be fine.

Anna doesn't move.

Liz You'd like some ice in it.

Toby Please. (*to Anna*) Yes please, lots of ice.

Anna nods, but has not understood.

Liz Squash, Anna.

Anna Squash.

Toby Well anything really. Anything soft.

Liz Look, I'd better go with her. I won't be a moment.

Liz and Anna go off. Toby involuntarily turns to watch Anna go.

Mike It's our perennial problem.

Toby (*turns back*) I'm sorry?

Mike Getting her dressed.

Toby Right.

Mike I mean getting her to get dressed. Not actually . . . dressing her.

Toby (*nods*) Right right. (*He takes out a cigarette.*)
,

I suppose she's in the bath a lot, or something.

Mike Because our major fear was naturally that her appearance would, well put people off.

Toby Yes?

Mike Only in that, she possibly creates the impression –

Toby (*lights up*) Well she wouldn't put me off quite frankly.

Toby laughs. Mike joins in. Brief laugh together.

Mike Listen, really we just wanted to thank you for everything you've done, and –

Liz (*coming out*) There's only lemon I'm afraid.

Toby No, that's fine.

Liz (*calls*) No, lemon's fine, Anna.
   It's surprising really just how limited her vocabulary actually is.

Toby She's French is she?

Mike Italian actually. Naples.

Liz It's the phone bills we dread.

Toby Well as long as it's not Australia.

   All faint laugh.

Liz Look, the thing is, is we just wanted to thank you for everything you've done, and –

   Anna enters with squash.

That's right, if you could just give it to Mr –

Toby Toby.

Liz I'm sorry. To Toby.

   Anna gives him the drink.

Toby Thanks.

   Anna returns to her book.

Liz Well, Cheers.

Toby Cheers.

Mike Cheers.

   '

Liz (*sotto voce*) Has she just had another bath?

Mike (*sotto voce*) I've really no idea what she's been doing.

Liz (*to Toby*) You can't imagine the trouble we've had getting her dressed.

Toby No, your husband was . . .

Liz I mean with people coming round to view all the time.

Mike (*jovial*) Well getting her to get dressed. Not actually getting her dressed.

Liz Well obviously not getting her dressed, Mike.

    '

Obviously she can dress herself.

Mike Look, is that cold enough for you?

Toby I'm sorry?

Mike No, sorry, I just thought for a moment there was no ice in it.

    Toby swirls the drink. The ice clinks.

Anyway, as Liz was saying, we just wanted to thank you for everything you've done, and . . . Well obviously we're delighted.

Liz (*laughs*) I mean the price was . . .

Mike (*laughs*) Well actually when you think about it it's quite ridiculous . . .

Liz Well the whole thing's ridiculous . . .

Mike It just stops meaning anything after a while . . .

Liz Because we'll be honest, we thought two hundred was probably pushing it, didn't we.

Mike The absurd thing is that we would almost certainly've taken less. Well particularly after . . .

Liz But two hundred and fifty . . .

Mike I know. It's crazy.

Liz It's quite crazy.

Mike I mean talk about spiralling . . . Two hundred and fifty. And cash.

Liz Well yes that's the amazing thing: cash.

Mike and Liz both chuckle. Toby looks on, swirling the ice in his glass.

Toby Yes, I feel we've achieved quite a favourable price. Although maybe not so remarkable for four bedrooms in the present climate. Of course the Baldwins had been recently disappointed by some vendors who had behaved – how shall we say? – rather less than honourably. (*all faint laugh*) So naturally the fact that you could offer them early possession was a strong point in your favour.

,

So . . . what exactly is your position now?

Liz Well naturally we're looking.

Toby And of course you are yourselves cash. Right. And your price?

Liz Well round about three hundred, isn't it.

Mike Well let's say we could be talking three-fifty for something exceptional.

Toby Three hundred and fifty. Right.

Liz The thing is, is we feel it's important to take our time.

Toby No, I understand that.

Mike (*laughs*) It's just some friends of ours . . .

Liz (*laughs*) Poor Poppy and Max . . .

Mike They panicked completely and ended up living on a railway.

They all laugh.

Mind you. It's quite a place. They've put in marble floors. Three bathrooms.

Liz Yes, but the trains . . . They're horribly overlooked, Mike.

Toby glances at his watch. Mike takes the bottle.

Mike Listen, you're sure you won't . . .

Toby covers his glass with his hand. Silence. Mike pours more wine for himself and Liz.

Liz (*laughs*) I think the thing is – isn't it – is that in a ridiculous kind of way we feel, well responsible.

Mike (*laughs*) Well responsible probably isn't the right word.

Liz No no, obviously not *responsible*.

Mike Because I think it would be wrong, I've said to Liz I think it would actually be morally wrong, for any of us to feel responsible, in that way.

Liz Well no, I don't mean responsible.

Mike Well you said responsible.

Liz Yes I know that's what I *said*, Mike.

Toby swirls his ice. He's looking at Anna.

Mike (*to Toby, with a note of aggression*) I mean, what do you feel?

Toby (*turns back*) I'm sorry? (*Looks at watch.*) Look, actually I ought to be . . .

Mike I mean my wife seems to feel we are, in some obscure way, responsible. So I just wondered –

Liz Please Mike.

Mike Look I just want to know what the man thinks for godsake.

,

Toby Well . . . (*faint laugh*) Surely if they . . . knew, if they knew about the railway when they bought it . . . then surely . . .

Mike The railway.

Toby Yes, if they knew about it when they bought it, then surely . . . unless there are . . . factors I don't know about. Then surely . . . well they can hardly hold either of you responsible for the purchase. (*Laughs.*) Can they?

,

Mike No no. You're quite right.

Toby Look, I'm afraid I have to –

Mike Go. Yes. Of course.

Toby It's just I've . . .

Mike Of course. No. We understand.

Toby I meant to be – very boring – meeting some people for a meal that's all.

Liz Well we're very grateful to you for dropping by.

Mike Yes. Thanks again.

Toby shakes hands with Mike and Liz.

Toby I'll see myself out.

Liz No. Please . . . (*Liz makes to go with Toby.*)

Mike The key.

They turn back.

Toby I'm sorry?

Liz Yes of course. Now it's all over – thank god – we meant to ask you for our key.

Toby The key.

,

Mike Well it doesn't have to be now. Whenever you can . . .

Toby No. Look. Sorry. I thought you'd . . . Because the thing is of course Clair had your key.

Mike Clair. Right. No. (*faint laugh*) Look, sorry.

Toby No no. Our fault entirely.

Liz Well it's hardly anyone's *fault*.

Toby (*on 'fault'*) No no. Obviously you must feel – well I think anybody would feel – because you're not the only people in this position, obviously. But yes I quite understand that you must feel there's a . . . question mark, if you like, over your security. Naturally the best thing would be to change the locks, but as you're moving out in a few days . . . Look. No problem. I'll speak to the Baldwins about it.

Mike But I'm sure it's –

Liz (*overlapping*) Please –

'

Toby No. Really. It's no trouble. I'll speak to them in the morning. (*about to go, with a nervous gesture to the garden*) They loved the vine.

Blackout.

GETTING ATTENTION

Getting Attention was first performed at the West Yorkshire Playhouse on 6 March 1991 with the following cast:

Milly Julia McCarthy
Bob Paul Slack
Sal Diana Hunter
Nick Nigel Cooke
Carol Adrienne Swan
Masked Figures/Painters John Axon, Graham Aggrey

Director Jude Kelly
Designer Robert Jones
Lighting Tim Thornally
Sound Mic Poole

Characters

Carol, early twenties
Milly, late fifties
Sal, late twenties
Nick, early thirties
Bob, mid twenties

First Masked Figure (male) who also plays
First Painter
Second Masked Figure (male) who also plays
Second Painter

The location is a small block of reasonably pleasant pre-war flats in South London. The time is the present

The stage is divided into three acting areas:

1   Extreme downstage, a small patch of grass representing Nick and Carol's garden

2   Remainder of stage, the living area of Nick and Carol's flat. A short passageway leads upstage to Sharon's bedroom door, with a glass panel over it. This door gives the impression of being buried deep in the flat, and may in fact be located beneath

3   The first-floor balcony with iron railings, which runs the length of the stage above the flat. The doors of Milly and Bob open onto this

Notes

Brackets ( ) indicate momentary changes of tone
(usually a drop in projection).

A comma on a separate line indicates a pause,
the exact duration of which must be determined
from the context.

Act One

SCENE ONE

Daylight on the balcony. Milly opens the door of her flat and shakes a tablecloth over the railings. A person in a gorilla-mask runs past, knocking lightly against her. As she recoils, a second masked figure knocks against her in pursuit of the first.

Milly Excuse me. (*louder*) Excuse me. Just what d'you think you're doing?

The two figures stop, turn deliberately, and stare at her.

Yes. What d'you two boys think you're doing up here?

They continue to stare without moving, then back away mockingly, in silence.

It's not funny you know. There's nothing funny about it at all. And don't think I don't recognise you. Because I know who you are, I know where you live.

The two figures go. Milly starts to shake the cloth again. A moment passes and Bob comes onto the balcony from the direction they've gone. He puts his key in the door.

Milly Did you see those boys?

Bob What's that, love?

Milly Those boys. The monkey.

'

Bob Didn't see anything, love. Sorry.

Bob opens his door.

Milly I know what I'd do with them if they were mine.

Bob Sorry love?

Milly I say, I know what I'd do with them. Because my Frank would've had his belt off to them, that's what he'd've done. And now it's in all the papers isn't it, you can't even smack a child, not in school. I mean if a teacher can't smack a child how're they going to learn what's right and wrong.

Bob (Well, I mean . . .)

Milly Well I'm sorry, but I think it's all wrong.

Bob is about to go in. Sal appears on the balcony.

Sal Hello, I'm looking for Number Six.

Bob What? Mitchell?

Sal Yes.

Bob You want the ground floor love.

Sal Thanks.

Bob enters his flat. Sal makes to go.

Milly They're not in.

Sal Sorry?

Milly Mitchell. They're not in.

Sal Right. Right, thanks.

Milly They went out at about quarter past. Well maybe a bit later. But it was before half past, I know that.

Sal Thanks.

,

Any idea when they'll be back?

Milly Well no they just all went off in his van. Well I call it his but of course it's his firm's, his firm's van.

Sal Right.

,

Listen, I must –

Milly Friend, are you?

Sal Sorry?

Milly You're a friend.

Sal Yes.

Milly Because they don't have many friends.

Sal Well I'm a friend.

Milly Although they seem very nice.

,

I don't know them at all but they seem very nice people. And of course the girl's quiet.

Sal Is she?

Milly Their little girl's very quiet, which is a blessing.

Sal Yes.

Both faint laugh.

Milly Got kiddies, have you?

Sal No.

Milly No, well there's still time.

,

Sal Listen –

Milly Teacher?

Sal . . . Mm?

Milly You a teacher, are you?

Sal (*faint laugh*) No.

Milly You look like a teacher.

Sal starts to go.

Sal Ground floor then.

Milly That's right. With the gardens.

Sal Right. Thanks.

Milly They're not in.

*Sal goes. Milly folds up her cloth and enters her flat.
A moment passes, then Sal reappears, the two figures
in rubber masks at a distance behind her. She stops,
they stop. She continues, they continue. She stops
again and turns. They stop.*

Sal (*sharply but frightened*) Fuck off. (*louder*) Look just
fuck off will you.

*They don't move. Bob opens his door and the figures
run off, unseen by him.*

Bob (*genial*) Still here then?

Sal (Just some idiots.)

Bob Mm?

Sal Just some idiots mucking about.

Bob Right. (*no idea what she means*) See you then.

*Bob goes off with a laundry bag. Sal remains on the
balcony. She lights a cigarette.
Blackout.*

SCENE TWO

Hammering can be heard. Then dim light comes up in the flat. Nick, bare-chested, is hammering at a bracket on the wall. On the balcony above, Milly's door clicks open a little way in the dark. Light behind the door reveals Milly, listening at the crack. Nick continues to hammer sporadically. Finally Carol comes out of Sharon's room, shutting the door behind her.

Carol Nick.

He continues.

Nick. You're going to wake her up, Nick.

He continues.

Nick.

Nick stops.

Nick What?

Milly's door closes slowly and clicks shut in the silence.

What? She asleep?

Carol Just gone.

,

Nick She eat her tea?

Carol Yeah.

Nick All of it?

,

All of it?

Carol She had all her juice.

Nick She didn't eat it then.

Carol She ate most of it.

Nick She's got to eat all of it.

Carol Well she did.

Nick (Like fuck.)

,

Carol (*brightly*) You got the aerial up?

Nick She's got to eat all of it.

Carol She had a pain.

Nick (I'll give her a pain.) She's got a pain because she doesn't fucking eat.

Carol Well you make her eat.

Nick She's not my kid. I know what I'd do with her if she was my kid.

,

(I'd make her fucking eat.)

Carol Well make her then.

Nick She's not my kid.

Carol She ate most of it.

Nick She's got to eat all of it. She's got to eat all of it if I'm living here.

,

(If she was my kid I'd have her say please and thankyou once in a while, yeah.) Manners.

Nick goes back to the wall and hammers. As he does so Milly's door on the balcony opens a crack as before, then a moment later, Bob's. Both are visible, listening.

Carol Can't you do it in the morning, Nick.

,

Nick, it's gone twelve.

Nick hammers. The glass panel over Sharon's door lights up.

You woke her up, you prat.

Nick drops the hammer. Carol goes into Sharon's room and shuts the door. Nick takes a television aerial from the floor and hooks it onto the bracket. In the silence the two doors on the balcony click shut. Carol comes out.

She wants her Care Bear.

Carol picks a teddy bear off the sofa. On her way back Nick intercepts her. They embrace. Carol gently frees herself.

She wants her Care Bear, Nick.

Carol returns to Sharon's room. Nick goes off to the kitchen. He comes back with a can of beer and surveys the aerial. Sharon's light goes out. Carol emerges and shuts the door. She puts her arms round Nick. A moment passes, the light comes on again.

Nick (Fuck.)

Carol What?

Nick indicates the glass panel. Carol gently breaks away. She goes into the room and emerges a moment later.

She wants her My Little Pony.

Nick Yeah?

*Nick looks for the toy. Although superficially
compliant he is growing more and more tense. He
picks up a green pony.*

Carol No, no, the pink one. She wants the pink one.

*Carol finds the pink pony and goes into Sharon's
room. Nick stands looking at the aerial, drinking from
the can. Sharon's light goes out and Carol emerges,
shutting the door. She comes up behind Nick and slips
her hands into his trouser pockets. They remain like
this for a while, backs turned, gently swaying.
Sharon's light comes on.*

Nick (Fuck.)

Carol Mm?

Nick (Fucking light.)

Carol She's alright.

,

Nick See what she wants. (*He breaks away*.) See what
she wants can't you. (What the fuck is it now?)

*Carol goes into the room again. A moment passes and
she comes out.*

Carol She wants a kiss.

Nick Well give her one. (Why's she telling me for
fucksake.) Give her one then.

Carol She wants you to do it.

Nick She wants me to do it.

Carol Yeah, she said she wants you.

Nick (*embarrassed*) (Fuck.)

,

Carol Well go on.

,

Nick She wants me to do it.

Carol Well go on.

Nick faint nervous laugh. He lights a cigarette.

Carol Well go on you prat. She wants you.

Nick goes into the room.

(And mind that cigarette.)

SCENE THREE

In the darkness the sound of Nick and Carol making love. Bob comes quietly onto the balcony lit only by the light from his partially open door. A corner of Milly's curtain is then drawn back, and Milly's face is visible, observing Bob, who sinks down, head pressed against the floor of the balcony. When the sounds die away, his breathing is audible in the silence.

SCENE FOUR

Daylight on the balcony.
  Carol appears.

Carol Oh. Hello.

Bob Hello. (Oh it's you. I was just . . .) I was just –

Carol I was looking for you actually.

Bob Yeah? Good. (Well what I mean is . . .) I mean I was just, yeah, I think I just dropped, dropped my key or something.

Carol Can you do us a favour?

Bob Or, well, I thought I heard it go, the key, but what I mean is, well is maybe it wasn't. So I, you know. (Thought I'd better have a look.)

Carol Yeah.

,

Look, can you do us a favour?

Bob Sure. (*He looks at the ground.*)

,

Carol What? You lost something?

Bob Yeah, well, no, I don't know actually.

Carol Can I use your phone then?

Bob Course. But look I'm sorry, course, you know you don't have to ask. It's just I've been disconnected. (*faint laugh*) I mean but look, er, come in, come in anyway. You want a coffee or something?

Carol Look, I need to make a phone-call.

Bob (Got this final demand.)

Carol I've got to ring someone.

Bob Right now, yeah.

Carol Yeah.

,

Yeah right now. Look –

Bob Well you better go down to the call-box.

Carol Yeah.

Bob Got a card?

Carol What?

Bob You got a card for the phone?

Milly (*opening her door to go out*) She's wasting her time with that call-box.

Bob I'll give you a card, alright.

Milly I say, you're wasting your time with it. Is it urgent?

Bob Yeah.

Milly Well she can use mine, you're welcome to use mine.

Carol Look, I . . .

Milly If it's a doctor or something you want is it.

Carol It's just my little girl. I just thought . . .

Milly What? Temperature?

Carol Temperature. Yeah.

Milly Been keeping you up with it has she. I thought I heard you up.

Carol is uncertain of Milly and becomes withdrawn.

You're welcome to use mine.

Carol Yeah.

'

Yeah, thanks. Look. I'd better get back.

Milly Don't you want to phone?

Carol (She's all on her own down there, that's all, she's all on her own.)

Milly Well I'll go down and mind her if you like, I don't mind.

Carol No, it's alright. It's alright thanks.

,

Look, I'd better get back.

Milly Well we could phone. We could phone for you.

Carol (No. She's . . .) She's alright.

Milly You sure?

,

Well yes you'd better get back then. It doesn't do to leave them, does it.

Carol No. (*She starts to go.*)

Bob I'll come down some time about my TV, if that's . . .

Carol (*without turning*) Yeah. Any time.

   Carol goes.

Milly There's a lot of that going round.

Bob Mm?

Milly That virus.

,

It wasn't your door key was it?

Bob Mm?

Milly You haven't lost your front door key.

Bob (*faint laugh*) No.

   Dim light up in the flat below. Nick is sitting watching TV, no sound. Carol enters the flat. Nick doesn't move.

Milly You ought to leave a spare with me. I'm normally in.

Bob Haven't got one.

Milly You should get one cut. Because I'm normally here.

> *Carol takes a cigarette out of Nick's shirt pocket and lights it. Nick takes no notice of her.*

Milly Spend your life running round after them don't you.

Bob Mm?

Milly Kiddies. That's why we never had any.

,

Yours keeping alright?

Bob You know . . . (*faint laugh. He looks away.*)

> *Carol sits at the table. She runs her hand over her face and through her hair before becoming still and staring out.*

Funny isn't it, I don't like to see a girl out without tights on, do you.

> *Bob faint laugh.*

Frank used to say it makes you wonder what else they've gone and left off. (*both faint laugh*) He was a devil, Frank. (*Milly goes.*)

> *Bob goes back inside. The lights fade on Carol and Nick.*
> *The two figures in rubber masks run onto the empty balcony. With a flamboyant display of skill they execute a picture in spray-paint on the wall between Bob and Milly's doors – either a cryptic 3D-effect*

*word (their personal signature) or perhaps a Disney
animal (Mickey Mouse). When complete, they admire
their work for a moment, then race away.*
Blackout.

SCENE FIVE

*Faint night-time light on the empty balcony, the painting
clearly visible. In the flat below Nick sits in front of the
soundless TV, which is the only source of light. Bob
stands beside him.*

Nick (*not looking at Bob*) Sounds like your decoder.

Bob I thought maybe it was the tube.

Nick But you got a picture.

Bob Yeah, well, you could call it a picture.

Nick (Snowstorm.)

Bob What?

Nick Snowstorm.

Bob That's right.

'

Nick What is it? Sony?

Bob Hitachi.

Nick Always goes on a Hitachi. Smoke?

Bob No thanks.

Nick (*lights up*) Damage your health.

Bob Sorry?

Nick Damage your health.

,

Bob I went to a hypnotist actually.

Sharon's door opens. Carol comes out.

Carol Oh. Hello.

Bob nods.

Nick Asleep?

Carol Yeah. (*She lies on the sofa with her head on Nick's lap. She kicks off her shoes.*) You want a beer? You asked him if he wants a beer Nick? (*She prods Nick.*) Nick, you asked him if he wants a beer?

Bob Thanks, but I've, well I've got to get back.

Carol Why didn't you ask him if he wants a beer?

Nick grins

You prat. (*She laughs.*)

Bob I better get back.

Carol See you then.

Carol's hand plays with Nick's face. She runs her fingers round the inside of his lips. Bob is embarrassed but too fascinated to move. Sharon's light comes on.

Bob So . . . when d'you reckon?

Nick (*looks at Bob for the first time*) What's that mate?

Bob When d'you reckon you can do it?

Carol She's put her light on again.

Nick Mm?

Carol She's put that light on again.

Nick Hey. Turn that light off.

Nick tenses and is about to get up when the light goes off. He relaxes. Carol puts her head back on his lap.

Bob The end of the week d'you think.

Nick What's that mate?

Bob You reckon you could do it by the end of the week.

Nick I thought I said take the bulb out.

Carol It's too hot.

Nick Sure. End of the week's fine.

Carol You want a beer?

Bob How's the temperature?

Carol Eh?

Bob Gone down?

Nick Well wrap something round it.

Carol You bloody well wrap something round it.

Bob What, doesn't she sleep?

Carol I'm not burning my fingers on that bulb.

,

Bob Can't she sleep?

Nick (Hyperactive mate.)

Bob Yeah?

Nick Fucking hyperactive. Won't eat. Won't sleep.

Bob Yeah? One of mine didn't sleep. You know, up in the night. Gets to you in the end.

Carol You got kids then?

Nick He's been to a hypnotist.

Carol Have you?

Bob faint laugh, embarrassed.

Carol What's it like?

Bob Well it's . . .

Carol I told Nick he ought to go, didn't I Nick, if he wants to give up.

Bob Well look I can let you have the name if you like when you come to fix –

Carol You prat!

Nick's ash has fallen onto Carol's leg. She jumps up and crosses to the other side of the room. She hitches up her skirt and examines her leg. Loud and angry, she is completely unselfconscious in front of Bob.

Carol You've burnt me you fucking prat.

Nick (*takes no notice*) I think I've got some in the van.

Bob watches Carol.

I think I've got some of those Hitachis –

Carol I'm going to have a scar you prat.

Sharon's light comes on.

Bob Well, you know, there's no hurry.

Nick No, I've got some Hitachis in the van.

Bob Great that's great.

'

(Well I'll . . .) I'll be on my way then.

Carol Look at it. Look at it, Nick.

Nick See you then.

Carol (Shit.)

Bob Right. Thanks.

,

(*He notices the light.*) End of the week then.

Carol You bastard.

Bob (*trying to be helpful*) Looks like she's awake again.

Carol You did that deliberate you bastard. You saw: he did that deliberate.

Bob I say, I think she's awake.

Carol You need treatment, you know that. People like you need treatment.

,

You going to apologise? Nick. You going to apologise to me?

,

Nick (*softly, without looking at Bob*) Tell her she can fuck off.

Carol Don't tell me to fuck off. (*louder*) Don't you tell me to fuck off.

,

Nick (*as before*) Tell her she's a cunt.

,

Milly appears on the balcony. She stops for a moment in front of the dimly-lit graffiti, then enters her flat.

*Nick gets out cigarettes. He offers the pack to Bob,
who declines. Nick lights up.*

(Damage your health.)

Bob (*faint laugh*) Yeah.

,

D'you think maybe it's additives? Because there's a link
isn't there. They've found a link, haven't they, between
additives and, you know, hyperactive.

*Milly comes out with a bucket and starts to scrub the
wall.*

Because nobody knows what half of them are, do they,
some of these additives.

Nick and Carol both silent and withdrawn.

Actually I think I will. I say I think I will have one if you
don't mind.

Nick Mm?

Bob Cigarette. If you don't mind.

*Nick hands him the pack. Bob lights up. He exhales
noisily and tries to look relaxed. Blackout in the flat.
On the balcony Milly continues to scrub, but makes
no impression. Bob appears, cigarette in hand.*

Bob (*jovial*) Busy then?

*Milly stops scrubbing. Both look in silence at the
picture.*

You won't get it off with Flash.

He notices that Milly is upset.

Why don't you leave it till morning. (*softly*) Why don't
you leave it till morning love.

Milly resumes scrubbing. Bob turns the other way and leans on the railings. He's about to take a drag of the cigarette, but then feels disgusted and scrunches it out with his shoe. Blackout.

SCENE SIX

The garden. Carol is stretched out, a drink beside her. Sal sits next to her on the ground. Both are watching Sharon playing at the far end of the garden – i.e. out into the auditorium. Daylight also on the empty balcony.

Carol She's just had a virus actually.

Sal She looks well though.

,

(*brightly*) Look, I'd like to meet Nick some time.

Carol Shal. Shal, get that out of your mouth. Get it out. Now. She keeps doing that.

Sal I say. I'd like to meet Nick.

Carol Just spit it out. Come on, spit it out.

,

He's out in the van.

Sal Yes, but if we could arrange a time.

Carol Well any time. Come round any time. (*faint laugh*) He'd kill her if he saw her doing that.

Sal It's just naturally I'd like to see you both together.

Carol Well he'll be back soon.

Sal I'll have to go quite soon.

,

Carol She's really happy out here. She always goes down the end like that and starts digging. There's holes all over down there.

,

Nick got her these bulbs. She dug them all up.

,

Your kids ever eat mud?

Sal I haven't got any.

Carol I suppose it's a phase.

Sal She's doing it again.

Carol Mm?

Sal She's doing it again.

Carol Sharon. What did I just tell you.

Sal faint laugh at Sharon.

Don't give me none of that cheek either.

,

She's getting cheeky like that with Nick sometimes. You know, I think she likes, you know, she likes winding him up.

,

Sal (*lightly*) How d'you mean?

Carol (Oh, you know, she's just . . .) difficult with him sometimes. He's very good about it actually.

,

(It's just sometimes when we want to . . . you know, going to bed . . .) She's not very good about going to bed.

,

125

Sal She'll need a lot of attention at the moment.

Carol Well she gets it. She –
Shal, just cut that out. Cut it out. (She's a devil.)

Both laugh at Sharon.

Sal How would a Thursday suit you?

Carol Thursday.

Sal Yes. Can I see you both on a Thursday afternoon?

Carol Any time, yeah.

Sal Thursday week?

Carol Course, I'll have to ask Nick.

Sal Well we can pencil it in.

Carol Mm?

Sal We'll, we'll say Thursday week unless Nick can't manage it. If Nick can't manage it maybe one of you would give me a ring would you.

Milly comes out onto the balcony to shake out a tablecloth.

Carol Well look, he'll manage it.

Sal (*lightly*) How d'you mean, winds him up?

Carol Nick? (*She looks away.*) Oh. You know. It's a phase. Things like food and things.

Sal How d'you mean?

Milly (*calls down*) Hello. Hello.

They turn.

Hello. I think your little girl's got something in her mouth.

Carol (*turns back*) (It's mud.)

Milly I think maybe she's eating something she shouldn't.

Carol (Yeah. It's mud.)

Milly (*to Sal*) You found her then.

Sal smiles.

Milly It looked like there was something in her mouth. You can never be too careful can you.

Carol Shal, spit it out.

Milly At least it's a bit warmer today.

Carol (*low, intense*) Shal. Shal, you want me to tell Nick? You want me to tell Nick when he gets in?

Milly Because I do feel sorry for them when they can't go out. Because there's nothing worse is there, than being cooped up indoors.

Carol (*as before*) Shal.

Milly It's a lovely age isn't it. I always think that's a lovely age for them.

Milly waits a moment for a conversation, then turns away.

Sal Look, I have to go.

Carol What, you got to go?

Sal I can't really wait any longer.

Carol He won't be long.

Sal I must go.

Carol He's really very good, you know, round the house. He's done the taps. Fixed the hot water.

Sal gets up to go.

Ever see him do you?

Sal Sorry?

Carol Her dad.

,

Sal No. No I don't. But, well I know who does see him. If you want me to pass on a message or something.

Carol Yeah. (Just tell him he's a cunt will you.)

They both laugh quietly together.

Sal Right. I must go.

Sal goes. Carol drinks. This is observed by Milly, who then goes indoors.

Carol Don't wipe it on your dress, Shal.

,

Carol hitches up her skirt to get the sun. She examines the burn on her thigh. Bob comes out onto the balcony. Carol stretches out again and slips the straps off her shoulders. Bob leans over the railings to watch. A long silence. Carol shifts a little. Nick appears on the balcony with an electrician's toolbox, unnoticed by Bob.

Nick Nice afternoon for it.

Bob Yeah. (*embarrassed laugh*)

Nick You in?

Bob Yeah. Sure. (I'm just . . .)

Nick I got your module.

Bob Great that's great.

Nick You in now are you?

Bob Well yeah, if it's convenient.

Nick No problem mate. You did say Sony?

Bob Hitachi.

Nick Yeah. Hitachi. Same thing. Japanese. No problem.

Bob Right.

Nick Whack it in now. Call it fifteen to you mate. That's cost, alright.

Bob Yeah that's very, that's very reasonable.

As Bob has edged away from the railings, Nick has moved nearer. He now notices Carol.

Nick Carol. Carol.

She looks up.

Cover yourself up.

Carol What?

Nick You seen that down there?

Bob What's that?

Nick It's a fucking striptease. Cover yourself up can't you. She thinks she's in fucking Tenerife. (Fuck.) Cover yourself up.

Grudgingly, ignoring Nick, Carol turns onto her stomach and covers her thighs a little.

You seen that down there?

Bob No? What's that?

Nick (Thinks she's in fucking Tenerife.)

Bob Yeah?

,

Growing up isn't she. Your little girl. I was just, just watching her playing out there.

Nick She's not my kid.

,

Bob No, no I know that. I just mean –

Nick Not mine mate.

Bob Still . . . It's a nice age.

,

You ever get birds down there?

Nick How's that?

Bob In your chimney. You know, birds in your chimney.

Nick No. Why's that?

Bob Often get them up here. Just wondered if they ever, you know if you ever get them down there at all.

Nick Birds. (*He looks at Bob.*)

,

Bob Yeah.

Nick No. No mate.

They start to go in.

Bob So, when you going?

Nick Where's that?

Bob Tenerife.

Both laugh. They enter Bob's flat.
Blackout.

SCENE SEVEN

*Night-time light on the empty balcony. Dim light in the
flat below. Nick is wrapping a toy.*

Nick She eaten it yet?

        ,

She eaten it yet?

Carol She had a bit.

Nick She's got to eat it all.

Carol Nick.

Nick She wanted it, she's got to eat it all.

Carol It's four days Nick.

Nick (Quicker she eats it then, yeah.)

Carol I told her.

Nick You told her I said.

Carol She knows.

Nick She wanted it.

Carol I know she did.

Nick (Well then.)

Carol She knows Nick.

        ,

It's four days it's been.

Nick Put it in the fridge.

Carol It's in the fridge.

Nick Well it will keep.

Carol (It doesn't keep does it.) You know it doesn't keep.

Nick Well cover it. Haven't you covered it?

Carol Can't we forget it.

Nick Haven't you covered it?

,

(Well I'll fucking cover it.) (*He gets up.*)

Carol Nick.

Nick I'll fucking cover it then.

> *Nick goes out to the kitchen. Carol toys absently with the wrapping paper. Nick returns.*

It stinks in there. Why didn't you cover it?

Carol Haven't I?

,

(*tentatively*) I was thinking about a microwave. Love. Nick. I say I was thinking about a microwave. I mean what I mean is is if we had a microwave, then you know, when she left it we could do it in the microwave. Because it only takes a minute in there. And I thought it would be, you know, more appetising, more appetising for her. When it'd gone and got cold I mean. Because it's not appetising for her when it's cold Nick. That's why I thought, you know, maybe we should get one.

Nick What, a microwave. (*He does not dismiss the idea.*)

Carol I was thinking about it, yeah.

,

Because every time I get the plate out and it's cold you know she just screams at me Nick, she just won't, she just won't. (That's why I thought, you know –)

Nick A microwave.

Carol Yeah, with a timer. She hits me Nick.

Nick She wanted it.

Carol I know she did, but she hits me.

Nick Well I'll talk to her then.

Carol Don't Nick.

Nick If she hits you I'll talk to her.

Carol Don't talk to her now.

Nick (If she fucking hits you.)

Carol Something like fishfingers only takes a minute.

Nick (If she fucking hits you I'll talk to her.)

Carol Then there's a bell. It's got a bell.

Nick She's disturbed, you know that?

Carol Who?

Nick Sharon. She's disturbed.

Carol No she's not. You don't know what you're talking about.

Nick She's like one of those kids. You know: Down's. She's a fucking Down's.

Carol Piss off.

'

You piss off.

Nick Fucking is.

Carol (Just piss off.)

Nick Won't eat. Won't sleep.

,

Carol She's a normal kid, Nick. She's perfectly normal.

Nick Wets herself.

Carol (*loud*) She's normal, Nick.

Nick So why's she got no pants on?

Carol What?

Nick Out in the garden. Why's she got no pants on out in the garden?

Carol She did have.

Nick (Disturbed, yeah.) See what I mean? Got no pants on. And there's, you know, our friend, there he is looking at her.

,

Carol (What? Bob?)

Nick Yeah. Bob.

,

There he is looking at her.

,

Carol You mend his set?

Nick And she's leading him on, that's the thing. She's leading him on.

Carol She's only a baby, Nick.

Nick That's what I mean.

,

(Disturbed.) (*He lights a cigarette. His mood lightens.*) (Then of course he says he's skint doesn't he.) Catch.

Nick tosses the wrapped present. Carol just catches it.

Carol Prat.

They both laugh. A heavy thump like a fall is heard.

That Shal?

,

Nick It's upstairs.

Carol You sure? (*She looks towards Sharon's door.*)

Milly comes out onto the balcony. She goes to Bob's door and rings.

Shal? You alright?

Nick She's asleep.

Carol Shut up. (*She listens.*)

Milly rings again. Bob opens his door. He's drunk.

Bob Yeah?

Nick I told you: she's asleep.

Milly Sorry . . . I just . . . Are you alright are you?

Bob (*bitter*) What's the problem love? Full of the joys of spring, yeah.

Nick It's upstairs. It's him.

Carol Shut up. (*She listens at Sharon's door.*)

Milly I just, well it sounded like somebody falling, that's all.

135

Bob Yeah. Me.

Milly I didn't mean to disturb you.

Bob It was me love. (*He grins alarmingly.*)

   Sharon's light comes on.

Nick I thought I said take that bulb out.

Bob Having a party.

Milly I didn't realise.

Bob No. No you didn't.

Nick I thought I told you to take that bulb out didn't I.

Milly You've . . . you've cut your eye.

Bob Yeah? (*He fingers his eye without concern.*)

Nick Well didn't I.

Carol She must've fell out, Nick.

Nick She can't've fell out if she put on the light.

Carol She must've.

Bob (*holds up his fingers and grins*) Blood.

Nick (*calls*) Turn that light off. (Told her to take it out didn't I.)

Carol Where's the key, Nick?

Nick Turn it off.

Carol Nick, where's her key? What you done with it?

Nick (I don't know.) (*He feels his pockets.*)

Milly I was just worried you'd hurt yourself or something.

Bob Well I did.

Bob grins. Milly laughs uncertainly.

Yeah. Well. Look. Thanks.

Carol You sitting on it?

She makes Nick get up.
  Milly is about to go back.

Bob You ever get birds?

Milly Sorry?

Bob Or is it just me?

,

Come in if you want. Having a party after all.

Carol finds the key. She unlocks Sharon's door and goes in, closing it behind her.

I mean it's not every day, is it, you get to enjoy yourself.

Milly (*with nervous brightness, an excuse to go back*)
I'm just in the middle of that film actually.

Bob What? *Evil Dead*? You watch that sort of thing?

Milly Well . . . you know . . . company isn't it.

Bob Company? Can't stomach that sort of thing.
Myself. Violence.

Milly Can't you? Oh I'm afraid I like a bit of violence.
Keeps me awake a bit of violence. (*faint nervous laugh*)

,

Bob Cheers then.

Milly Goodnight.

Bob stares at Milly as she goes back. Their doors close simultaneously.

,

Sharon's light goes off. Carol comes out, looks at Nick, sits down.

Nick You locked it?

,

(*Snaps fingers.*) Key.

Nick takes the key from Carol and locks Sharon's door. Blackout. A faint intermittent scratching sound becomes audible, like a bird trapped in a confined space. Nick lights a cigarette in the darkness. He sits and turns the TV on, no sound. The television is the only light, lighting up his face close to the screen. Time passes. Carol comes in.

Carol I thought you was Shal.

,

Nick (*without looking at her*) (Can't sleep.)

,

Carol goes and sits beside Nick. He stares at the screen.

Carol (*softly*) I thought you were going to stop.

Nick inhales.

I thought you said you'd stopped, Nick.

Carol snatches the cigarette out of Nick's mouth. Nick looks at her.

Nick It's a habit. (Once you start . . .)

Carol begins to smoke the cigarette.

Carol You said you'd stopped.

Nick I have stopped.

,

138

(*with difficulty*) Look. What I want. All I want. Is some respect. (Yeah, respect.) When I say good morning, I want her to say good morning. When I say, please eat that, I want her to eat it. Because if I live here. (I mean I am living here.)

,

I'm talking about respect that's what I'm talking about.

Carol She's just a baby, Nick.

Nick (Like there was something wrong with me.)

,

Carol Just you said you'd stop.

Nick I have stopped, I'll stop when she stops.

,

Carol (*strokes Nick's hair*) I ordered it Nick. A microwave.

Nick doesn't react.

It's a nice one. Coffee-coloured. You'll like it. Make a big difference Nick.

Blackout.
The scratching sound fades away.

SCENE EIGHT

Daylight on the garden and balcony. In the garden Nick, bare-chested, is doing exercises with a piece of portable apparatus, watched from the balcony by Milly, who is pegging out washing. Carol appears and rings Bob's bell.

Milly You're wasting your time there.

Carol glances at Milly. She rings again.

He's making me feel quite exhausted. I say: your husband's making me quite out of breath up here.

Carol rings again.

Mind you there's nothing worse is there, than a weedy man. My husband was wiry like that. And my god he could lift. There was nothing that man couldn't lift.

Carol rings again.

He's sleeping it off in there. You're wasting your time.

Carol (*calls down*) Nick. Nick he's not in.

Nick looks up.

He must've gone.

Milly (*to Carol*) He's definitely in.

Nick Where's he gone?

Carol He's out.

Nick You tried again?

Carol He's not in.

Milly (*to Carol*) He is.

Carol What?

Milly He is in. Just he's not answering.

Nick Try it again.

Milly You won't get an answer.

Carol She says he's not answering, Nick.

Nick Try it.

Carol rings.

,

What, is he out then?

Carol Must be.

Milly (*calls down to Nick*) He's not.

Nick What?

Milly He's not out.

Nick Well where is he then?

,

I thought you said he was out.

Carol I thought he was, Nick.

Nick Well she just said he's not.

Carol I know she did.

Milly Well I suppose he might be. I mean he might be but I don't think he is. I think he's sleeping it off.

Carol What shall I do Nick? Nick what d'you want me to do?

Nick turns away and resumes exercises.

Milly If you want to use a phone there's always mine.

Carol about to go.

You want me to give him a message if I see him? I usually see him.

Carol Can you just tell him Nick wants that money.

Milly Owes him money does he?

Carol about to go.

Haven't seen your little girl today.

Carol (No.)

141

Milly Not ill again is she?

'

It's knowing what to do with them isn't it. My niece has got three and she says it's terrible in summer knowing what to do with them. Hers like the zoo but you can't keep going to the zoo can you. Have you been to the zoo?

Carol No.

Milly Of course, they're vegetarians.

Nick leaves the garden.

You look tired. Been keeping you up has she. Thought I heard you up.

Have you been to a doctor about her diet? Because her youngest, they had terrible trouble with him, and it turned out he was allergic. So maybe she's not getting the right additives or whatever it is it's meant to be now. Because of course you have to be firm with them too. My niece says she loves them but you have to be firm with them or your life's not your own. I mean I'll be perfectly honest with you that's why Frank and I never had any because we wanted our own life. He had so many things planned for when he retired. You wouldn't believe the things he had planned.

'

They must be the same age, yours and her youngest. I think that must be a difficult age, three. Mind you Kerry says it's always a difficult age. (*faint laugh*) She ought to know.

'

Carol (She's not three.)

Milly Isn't she? I thought she was. I thought you said she was.

Carol She's four.

Milly Four is she? I thought she was three. Well of course, you must know.

Carol Today. Four today.

Milly That's nice. Mind you it always ends in tears doesn't it.

'

You doing anything nice? Why don't you go to the zoo. Since he's home with the van. I say: why don't you go to the zoo or something since you've got your husband home with the van.

Carol He's not my husband.

Milly Well common-law isn't he. I mean it's only a piece of paper after all.

> *Carol looks away and bites her lip. She seems to be on the verge of saying something.*

Is it your head? D'you want something for it?

> *Nick reappears in the garden.*

Nick (*calls up*) Carol.

Milly I've had some terrible heads since I've been living here. I'm wondering if it's asbestos, some asbestos we've not been told about.

Nick Carol. You're wanted.

Carol Can't you do it Nick.

Nick She wants you. She's asking for you.

Milly (*worldly-wise*) It's attention isn't it.

Carol looks in despair at Milly.

The more you give them, the more they want.

,

Nick You coming or what.

Carol hesitates a moment, then goes. Once he sees Carol on her way, Nick leaves the garden. Milly is about to go in when Bob's door opens and Bob appears with a terrible hangover. They remain suspended for a moment, Milly about to go in, Bob about to come out. Bob groans.

Milly She's gone.

,

Just this minute.

,

I said you wouldn't want to talk to anyone.

Bob clutches the railings and leans over.

You been sick have you?

Bob (No.)

Milly Well maybe you ought to try. Have you tried?

,

(It's these mornings you really miss having a garden isn't it. The smell of it first thing. Mint by the back door. I always used to have mint handy by the back door.

,

Because they don't look after them do they. Let's face it, they don't.)

,

D'you want something for that head?

Bob groans assent.
Milly goes inside. Bob puts his hand to his head
and squints against the light. The voices of Nick and
Carol become very faintly audible: laughing and
giggling punctuated by silences. Milly comes out with
tablets and a glass of water.

(Thanks.) (*He drinks and hands the glass back.*) Thanks.

Milly You're welcome.

Blackout.

SCENE NINE

In the darkness the voices of Nick and Carol grow
louder. Nick is laughing, encouraging; Carol, also
laughing, but throughout the scene swinging between
extremes of mood, is trying to resist Nick – 'No Nick.
Leave it out.' etc.
The panel over Sharon's door lights up. Then, in
response to the commotion, Milly's door clicks open, and
she is visible, listening at the crack, followed a moment
later by Bob at his own door (cf Scene Two).
Finally the light comes on in the flat, revealing on
the table a cake with four unlit candles, surrounded
by beer-cans. Nick and Carol enter. Nick is wearing a
rubber 'joke' mask, and trying to make Carol wear
one too.

Carol No Nick. Come on, leave it out. That's Sharon's.
Leave it out. (*more emphatic*) Leave it out Nick.

,

Alright alright. (Bloody thing.) Bloody thing Nick.

Nick puts the mask on Carol. Both giggle.

Mind out Nick. Mind my face.

Nick adjusts the mask roughly.

You're hurting me Nick. Nick.

Nick finishes adjustments. He steps back. Both giggle.

It's hot in here. I'm going to get too hot.

Nick blows a paper roll-out squeaker. Carol giggles. He stalks her round the room.

I won't tell you what that reminds me of.

More of the same business. Nick presses her against the table. Some cans fall.

You're meant to be lighting the candles.

Nick presses against her. He says something inaudible. She shrieks with laughter.

Nick you're meant to be lighting the candles.

Nick presses more intimately against her.

Leave it out Nick. I don't like old men.

Nick persists.

(*more emphatic*) I said I don't like old men. (*She slips away.*) Where's them matches?

Nick snatches them off the table.

Give me them matches, prat. (*She laughs.*)

Nick passes the box repeatedly from one hand to the other behind his back as Carol tries to grab them. They laugh. Carol gets the box and moves away.

(Daft bastard aren't you.)

Carol lights the candles. Nick makes a blowing sound.

Prat. (*brief laugh*)

'

Let's have the present now. Come on. Give us her present you prat.

Nick picks up the present. Repeatedly he pretends to throw it to Carol, who makes to catch it, laughing nervously. Finally Nick tosses the present wide, and it falls to the floor. Carol picks it up and feels it.

(It's broken.) You've broken it you prat.

Nick begins to laugh. Carol pulls her mask off.

You've broken it.

Unable to resist Nick's laughter, Carol also laughs at length, but finally stops and bites her lip.

Don't let her see it.

She gives it to Nick, who pushes it under the sofa with his foot.

Shal. Shal, you coming out? You coming out for your cake?

'

You coming out for your cake, Shal? (What's she doing in there?)

Nick pulls his mask off.

Don't you want to try your Funny Face Nick's gone and got you, Shal? Aren't you going to blow your candles out?

'

Nick You coming out of that fucking room or d'you want fetching out?

Carol (Nick . . .)

Nick You come out here and eat this fucking cake your mum's gone and bought.

Carol Aren't you going to blow your candles out?

Nick I'm counting to three.

,

Carol You heard what Nick said, Shal. You heard what he said.

,

Nick One. (*He opens a can of beer.*)

Carol (Nick . . .)

Nick Two.

Carol (Please Nick . . .)

> She turns. Nick is sprinkling beer over the cake. The candles go out. Both begin to laugh. Nick presses against her.

Nick (Three.)

Carol Prat.

> She puts her arms around him.
> Blackout.

Act Two

SCENE ONE

Daylight on the balcony and garden where Carol lies, sunbathing, but fully dressed. A moment passes. She shifts a little and lies still again. Milly comes out of her flat, closing the door behind her. She goes straight to the railings and begins to speak, her manner at the same time nervous and defensive.

Milly Quite often, yes.

Well I wouldn't say friendly terms exactly. I mean what I mean is, well out in the garden.

I'm sorry?

Well from my balcony. My balcony overlooks their gardens you see. (*fast*) Because of course the fact was, when we moved in it was on the understanding we'd be allocated those gardens, but of course we never were, and then they moved these families in, and of course they got the gardens didn't they, on account of the children. I mean it's little wonder really there's trouble with those sort of families.

I'm sorry?

Well I was just giving my opinion that's all.

Change of tack in questioning.

Well that depends what you mean by reason to suppose. Because of course you know she drank.

Mrs Mitchell yes. She normally had a bottle out there, in the urn.

Well a kind of ornamental urn. And another down by the fence. And . . . well . . . well it's all very well in the Bahamas isn't it. What I mean is, well, she was often,

149

you know, topless out there. And I've nothing against it personally if you've got the figure for it, but there's a time and a place isn't there, and I thought that was, well, unnecessary, you know, for the child, to see her mum like that.

    Carol shifts a little and lies still.
    Change of tack.

Well only out in the garden as I say.
    (*becoming upset*) Well she was a very quiet child. I don't think I ever heard her . . . well I don't think I ever heard her speak now I come to think of it. She was what I call mousey, d'you know what I mean, a mousey sort of child. Mostly she used to dig up the border at the end with a spoon which was a shame because it could've been a nice border . . . plenty of sun . . . (*She breaks off.*)
    No nothing like that. But her clothes weren't very clean, you know. Always the same yellow dress. (*faint laugh*) (That yellow dress . . .) And it wasn't as if they were hard up particularly because she had plenty of things. I mean nearly every Friday he brought something home for her.
    Taylor. Yes.
    Well I used to see him getting out of his van and he nearly always had something so it can't've been as if they were particularly hard up although it's true they weren't on the phone, although of course there was the microwave, but what I mean is is it was always the same dress, which worried me. And of course sometimes they let her put mud in her mouth.
    Yes. Mud. She was eating it. I used to think to myself for heaven's sake what's wrong with giving her a good hot bath once in a while. (I'd've done it myself given half the chance.)

    Carol drinks.

Well of course there was cause for concern, of course
there was, (particularly knowing what we do now), but
I mean what right would I 've had to go interfering,
that's the thing. And naturally, well I naturally assumed
that people like that, a family like that, they'd be on the
list, the register, whatever it is. I mean surely someone
ought to be keeping an eye on a family like that.

Yes I did. But I would've been frightened to say
anything personally, because of him.

Taylor, yes. Particularly knowing what we do now.

Carol lies down again.

Well no, maybe not at the time, but I'm talking about
what we know now. (I mean how anyone could do those
things to a child . . .)

Well I'm sorry but I don't see how you can say the
facts have to be established, because, well, surely we've
all read the papers. (And well it would make an angel
weep, wouldn't it, the things he did.)

Change of tack.

No I never paid them what you'd call a social visit.
(Although I did go collecting down there once because
of course since Frank went I do a lot of that for cancer,
you know.) And of course we often used to hear them,
especially when they first moved in . . .

(*embarrassed*) (Well, not so much arguments as . . .)

Yes, that's right. And I used to think, well if we can all
hear them, what must it be like for the child down there.
The person you really ought to speak to is my next-door
neighbour –

Yes. Mr Brook. Because he had dealings with them I
believe. Well I know for a fact he went down there quite
often, and, well, it amazes me quite frankly he didn't get
wind of something. I mean he must've been walking
round with his eyes shut.

Bob appears on the balcony, his arms round a bag of shopping.

(*with innuendo*) And of course sometimes she used to come up.

Mrs Mitchell, yes. Sometimes she used to call on him. In the day, do you see what I mean. Well of course I'm not blaming him, I'm not blaming him at all, because, (*confidential*) well, you probably know his wife went off with that Greek from the Pizza Hut and so he gave up his job to look after the children and then the social whatever started interfering and took them into care right over his head which broke his heart, didn't they. Because really I think they can go too far breaking a family up without a second thought like that, and so you can hardly blame him if he felt like a bit of company sometimes, although I can't say I approved of his choice, particularly knowing what we do now.

Bob enters his flat.

Well no, I couldn't say they definitely were, but then I wouldn't like to say they definitely weren't, do you see what I mean.

Change of tack.

Does she? Well maybe she tried to call a doctor from there if that's what she says, but I thought he'd been disconnected, because I knew he'd had a final demand and that was months ago.

And besides I remember now I did once offer her the use of the phone when he was out but she was quite insistent it was him she wanted to see. So that's what I mean when I say the phone was only, well, it was just a pretext in my opinion.

Blackout.

SCENE TWO

In the darkness the sound of intermittent scratching, just audible. Then faint light on the balcony, revealing Bob standing at the railings. In the flat below Sharon's light comes on. There is a chair in front of her door. Nick enters and switches on a light in the room. He puts a box on the table, takes out a broken toy (the present) and looks at the pieces, which he tries to fit together. The scratching persists.

Carol (*off*) Nick. Nick, peppers or ham-and-cheese?

,

Nick Peppers.

,

Carol (*off*) Ham?

Nick Peppers.

Bob Well at the time I thought it was a bird.
  Well yes, because although they sealed up our fireplaces they never bothered to cap the chimneys, and so you often get them in there. (It was one of the things used to drive my wife mad actually, you know, listening . . .) Because there's, well there's no way of getting them out.

Scratching persists. Nick fiddles with the toy.

Nick Carol. Carol I'll have ham.

Carol (*off*) I thought you said peppers.

Change of tack.

Bob Well I was very aware of when he first moved in there.

Yes. Mr Taylor. I was very aware of when, Mr Taylor, when he first moved in.

Well they used to be quite, well, noisy I suppose.

Carol (*enters*) I've just got out a peppers Nick.

Bob Yes, arguments. But not just arguments. I mean –

Nick Well peppers then. I'll have peppers.

Bob I'm sorry?

Carol Well I could get out a ham.

Bob Yes that's right. There used to be a lot of, yes, sexual noise. Well and arguments as well. Or at least I suppose they argued. But sometimes, to be honest, well sometimes, you know, you couldn't distinguish. (*faint laugh*)

Carol I could get out a ham, Nick.

Nick says nothing.

Bob Well that depends what you mean by average, doesn't it.

Carol goes back into the kitchen.

Well what I mean is, is I certainly heard them, both of them, raise their voices if you like to the child on occasion. And the child, well, she'd cry or whatever. But most of the time, well what I'm trying to say is, is most of the time there was nothing to suggest it was anything other than, you know, normal domestic, you know, whatever. (But of course knowing what we do now . . .)

Most of the time, yes. I mean I don't know about you, but I've got kids myself (or did have) and there are days aren't there, when you don't get a rest from them so they wind you up, they wind you up and in retrospect you realise maybe you've been a bit hard on them (whatever).

You know, you look at them when they're asleep, and you think well maybe I did go a bit far. That happens.

Carol returns, bringing the cutlery etc for Nick's meal. She lays a place at the table.
Change of tack.

That depends what you mean by reason to believe.

Well just once or twice, I mean only once or twice, it's true it sounded . . . (Well what I mean is . . .)

What I mean is once or twice maybe I did wonder exactly what was going on down there. And actually I had decided, if it happened again (well what I mean is is I'd thought about it) I did decide I'd go down (you know, and . . . whatever). But as it turned out, well it didn't happen again, so naturally I didn't.

(Yes yes pretty violent.)

(*with anger*) I said pretty violent. Yes.

Carol What's that noise Nick?

Nick What?

Carol That Shal?

Nick What noise?

They listen. The scratching has stopped. Silence. Carol resumes doing the table. Nick fiddles with the toy.
Change of tack.

Bob (Well no, I'm afraid that wouldn't've occurred to me.)

I say I'm afraid that wouldn't've occurred to me.

Well let's just say I've had, well, dealings, with those people before, and I'm afraid well that's just the last thing that would occur to me, I mean to get involved with them, voluntarily if you see what I mean.

Carol goes back to the kitchen.
Change of tack.

Bob (*with bitterness*) Yes they are. They are in care. But I don't see what business that is of yours actually.

Well yes it is (and of course it sounds stupid now doesn't it) but yes it's perfectly true I wouldn't want to be responsible for breaking up a family the way mine's been broken up if that's what you mean . . . Because I mean you're just . . . Well my own life has been . . . (Well.)

Silence.
Change of tack.

(Yeah, we were on friendly terms, yeah.) But the person you really ought to speak to is my next-door neighbour –

That's right. Mrs Austin. Because, well, she doesn't miss much. And actually it's a wonder to me she didn't get wind of something.

Oh yes I did go down. A couple of times maybe.

Well they were always, you know, very hospitable actually, very easy-going.

Knocking. Nick tenses.

No I wouldn't say I noticed any, what, tension did you say? No I wouldn't say there was any tension particularly down there, no. Well the opposite really. They both seemed very relaxed together. They just, well, got on with it really. Mr Taylor in particular was very relaxed, struck me as a very easy-going sort, which is why I wouldn't've thought he'd . . . well I still find it difficult to believe to be honest.

Knocking again. Carol appears. She looks at Nick.

He repaired my television as a matter of fact. (I still owe him for it actually.)

Knocking again.
Change of tack.

Yes she was there, but I didn't see her.

Nick gestures to Carol to answer the door. She does so.

Well she was asleep. She was asleep in her room.

Bob falls silent, but remains on the balcony.

Milly (*off*) Not if I'm disturbing you.

Carol (*off*) Course not. I'll just ask Nick.

Carol enters with Milly, who holds a collecting box.

Carol Got any change Nick?

Milly I don't want to disturb anybody . . .

Nick What for?

Carol What's it for?

Milly It's cancer. Cancer research.

Carol Cancer.

Nick Yeah?

Milly Look. I can, I can come back when it's more convenient.

Sound of microwave timer.

Carol Scuse a minute.

Carol goes out to the kitchen. Silence.

Milly I'm sorry, I didn't realise you were eating.

Nick I'm not love.

Milly faint laugh. Nick smiles.

Milly It's bigger than I thought.

Nick What's that?

Milly Down here.

,

Nick Yeah?

,

Yeah I could do with some of that.

Milly Sorry?

Nick Charity.

Milly faint laugh. Nick smiles.

Milly It's more than eighty per cent . . .

Nick Mm?

Milly Goes to research.

Nick nods. He is still holding the toy.

Otherwise I wouldn't do it.

,

She break it?

Nick Plastic. Can't do anything with it.

Nick tips the box to show Milly the pieces. One of the rubber masks falls out onto the floor.

Milly Thought I heard her crying.

Nick Yeah?

Milly bends down and picks up the mask. Carol enters with a pizza for Nick.

She been crying?

Carol Who?

Nick Shal.

Carol No.

They look at Milly, who is looking at the mask.

Milly Must've been someone else's. They don't like this hot weather do they. (*She drops the mask back in the box.*)

Nick What's this?

Carol It's ham.

Milly Poor little souls.

Nick Ham?

Carol I got one out.

Milly Asleep is she?

Carol It's alright isn't it?

Milly Is she asleep?

Carol What?

Nick Sharon.

Carol Oh. Yeah.

Nick (Makes a change.)

Milly (Must've been somebody else's.)

Nick starts to eat.

Carol Alright?

Nick nods.

Milly Well, look, maybe I'll come back when it's more convenient.

Carol (*embarrassed*) Haven't you given her anything Nick? (*louder*) Nick.

Nick gets up and looks for some change.

Milly I don't want his dinner to get cold.

Carol I can microwave it.

Milly Have you got a microwave then?

Carol Nick treated me. Didn't you love.

Milly That must be handy with the kiddy.

Carol Made a big difference. Come on. Sorry about this.
He's a bit slow sometimes. Aren't you love.

*Nick gives some change to Carol, who puts it in the
box. Milly peels off a sticker and sticks it on Carol's
dress. She peels off another and registers that Nick has
no shirt on. Embarrassment.*

Carol I keep telling him to cover himself up.

Milly (*faint laugh*) It's just, well, knowing where to stick
it.

*All three relieved laughter. Nick takes the sticker and
sticks it on his chest.*

Carol Nick . . .

*More laughter from Milly and Nick. Carol shows
Milly out. Nick goes back to his food.*

Milly (*off*) Bye.

Carol (*off*) Bye.

Carol reappears.

Nick She needs a bath.

Carol She's asleep.

Nick She smells. She's beginning to smell.

Carol gets onto the chair in front of Sharon's door and peers through the glass.

Carol (*faint laugh, with affection*) Doing a tortoise.

Blackout on flat.

Bob Well I quite often used to see . . . Mrs Mitchell . . . Carol, out in the garden. I mean she often used to, well she sunbathed a lot out there.

Drank? Well not particularly. Not more than anyone else I wouldn't've said.

Quite often I suppose. She did a lot of digging out there.

(*faint laugh*) Yeah, digging. (I suppose I thought that was odd sometimes, you know, for a girl.) But I will say, whenever I saw her –

Milly appears on the balcony with the collecting box. She passes behind Bob and goes into her flat.

Well not that often it's true. But whenever I saw her, the girl, well, you know . . . Well what I mean is, some of the things in the papers and so on I think they're a bit extreme –

Well maybe they're true, I don't know, but there are ways of putting things aren't there. I mean I don't believe she had to eat mud, I mean that's a lie I never saw her eat mud . . . (*His feelings about Carol are getting him into a mess.*) . . . because she was always (well as far as I could tell of course) but she was always, you know she looked clean and as if, you know, someone cared for her. (Though obviously . . .) And her mum too, well she was the same, she always took care of her appearance, you know, attractive to look at. And the girl . . . Well . . . You know . . . The same, attractive, attractive to look at, like her mum.

Blackout.

SCENE THREE

Daylight on the empty balcony. Two painters enter and set up their gear to paint out the graffiti.

First Painter Your first is it?

Second Painter Yeah.

,

First Painter Girl?

Second Painter Boy.

First Painter Yeah?

,

Second Painter Marcus.

,

First Painter Marcus.

Second Painter Yeah, well, my wife, she was looking for something a bit different, and, well, I like it too.

First Painter Yeah?

Second Painter Yeah. Yeah, nice name.

,

First Painter Different.

Second Painter Yeah that's right.

,

He . . . smiled this morning.

First Painter Marcus.

Second Painter Yeah. First time.

*He smiles at the recollection. First Painter is
embarrassed.*

He's got blue eyes. Because it's funny, you know, I
haven't got blue eyes, and Linda, well, she hasn't either,
then we found out, they've all got blue eyes, you know,
when they're born.

First Painter Yeah who told you that?

Second Painter In a book. Baby book we've got.

First Painter Baby book.

Second Painter Yeah.

,

What about you?

First Painter How d'you mean?

Second Painter You got kids?

First Painter faint laugh.

,

First Painter My sister had a mongol.

,

Second Painter Yeah?

First Painter (Fucking mongol, yeah.)

Second Painter They can test you for that now.

First Painter Thing is is it's like she doesn't realise. You
know she talks to it and everything like it's normal.
(Georgina.)

Second Painter (I don't think I could've . . .) I don't
think I could cope with that.

First Painter Her old man's gone off with a travel agent. Well, can't blame him, can you, mongol like that.

They start to paint out the graffiti with long-handled rollers.

You going anywhere?

Second Painter Holiday?

First Painter Yeah.

Second Painter (*faint laugh*) (Joking mate.)

,

You?

First Painter Tenerife.

Second Painter Yeah?

First Painter Two weeks. (She fixed it up for me actually.)

Second Painter Who's that?

First Painter His girlfriend. She fixed it up.

They continue to paint. Lights up in the flat below. Carol quiet but agitated. Nick, sitting in front of the soundless TV, is shocked and frightened.

Carol It's all of her legs. It's all of her legs Nick.

Nick (*quietly and deliberately*) I said to her: please. You heard me say to her, I said: please, Sharon, do what I say, just do what I'm fucking telling you for once. Please. I said please do what I'm fucking telling you. (I said: look I'll count to three.)

Carol Someone will see it you prat.

Nick (Fucking call me a prat.)

Carol (*loud*) Someone will see it.

Nick It's just her feet. It's nothing. It's just the soles, the soles of her feet. Nothing.

Carol How hot was it?

Nick (It wasn't hot.)

Carol (Well it must've been.) It must've been hot Nick.

Nick Of course it was fucking hot.

,

(*loud*) Well of course it was fucking hot, when did you last give her a wash give her a bath, no you left it to me, so I told you if you fucking well leave it to me to do it I'll do it my way, I'll do it my own fucking way and I'll have some respect because it's not my kid it's your fucking kid and you can make it eat and you can fucking clean it too. (Fucking call me a prat.)

> *As if in response to Nick's shouting, Bob and Milly open their respective doors simultaneously and come to the balcony rail. No interaction between them and the painters, who quietly continue their work.*

,

Carol What was it she said?

Nick (*quiet again*) She didn't say anything.

Carol I heard her say something Nick.

Nick (Too hot, she said it was too fucking hot.)

Carol I'm worried about her skin. We've got to get someone to come.

Nick (I said: look I'll count to three. She had fair warning.)

Carol She's only a baby Nick.

Nick (*loud*) She had fair warning.

,

Carol Have you seen her skin?

,

Someone's got to come.

Nick It's the soles. It's nothing. She's asleep isn't she.

Carol No she's not asleep Nick. She's not bloody asleep.

Nick Well she's quiet.

Carol I know she's quiet.

Nick Well.

Bob Well in the end it went very quiet down there. Yeah, I suppose that was the oddest thing really, thinking about it now. I mean they were rather less, you know, active, than they had been. And as I say, sometimes I noticed this kind of, well, scratching.
Yes like a bird.

Carol Couldn't you run the cold?

Nick I ran the cold.

Carol You said it was hot.

Nick She said it was hot. I never said it was fucking hot.

Carol You just said it was hot.

Nick Well I ran the cold, alright.

Milly Because it's not as if I didn't offer to go down there and babysit for a couple of hours if it would've helped. Because actually nothing would've made me happier than to give that poor kiddy a good hot bath and a change of clothes.

Carol heads for the door.

Well she was so vague, that's the thing. I mean one day she'd tell you the kiddy was three and the next she'd be telling you it was four. But then I suppose if you drink like that . . .

As Carol passes, Nick grabs her arm. They look at each other. Carol pulls free and goes out. Nick doesn't move.

Bob Yeah we were on friendly terms. I mean Carol . . . Mrs Mitchell, she came up once or twice –

Nick (Well fuck you.)

Bob I'm sorry?
How d'you mean, a relationship? I mean she just came up to use the phone that's all.
Does she? Well of course I never asked her why. I mean you don't do you.

Carol appears on the balcony, attracting the attention of the painters. She goes to Bob's door and rings.

Well maybe she wanted to call a doctor I don't know. But well, to be honest with you she can't've called anyone.
Well I mean I've been disconnected for a while now.
Distressed? No I wouldn't've said she was distressed particularly.

Carol begins to bang at Bob's door.

Well I know it's not very logical. I never said it was logical. I'm just telling you what she did.

First Painter (*amused at Carol's agitation*) Come on love. It might never happen.

Carol bangs again.

167

Milly Well I'm sorry but I disagree. Because the thing is, well what you've got to ask yourself is why people like that, why they're allowed to have children in the first place if they can't be bothered to look after them. Because let's face it, it's a simple enough thing in this day and age to tie up the tubes . . .

Carol heads past the painters for Milly's door.

. . . because my Kerry, my niece that is, she had it done after her third, and well, surely that would be kinder, to've done that in the first place before any of this could've happened.

Carol has difficulty passing the painters. First Painter assists her with mock chivalry.

First Painter You want to take it a bit easy love.

Carol starts to bang on Milly's door.

That banging's affecting my blood pressure. (*He winks at Second Painter.*)

Milly Well no it's quite true I never saw her being what you'd call maltreated by either of them but, well, I saw enough to draw my own conclusions, and surely we've all read the papers and so on and if you want my opinion the whole thing's criminal because we all know what happens . . .

Carol gives up. She passes again with difficulty past the painters.

. . . because what happens is they're put away aren't they, and then the next thing you know it's good behaviour and the rest of it and they're out and doing it all over again. Because life should mean life shouldn't it, or else why bother why bother at all.

I'm sorry?

Well I'm just giving my opinion that's all.

Carol leaves the balcony. A moment passes.

First Painter I could give her one, I really could.

,

Second Painter She'd eat you alive mate.

First Painter Yeah? Wouldn't mind.

*Painting finished, they begin to pack up. Carol
appears in the flat. Nick in the flat, Bob and Milly on
the balcony, do not move. Carol sits at the table. She
runs her hands through her hair. She stares out.
Blackout.*

SCENE FOUR

*Bright light up on all areas: the garden, which has
perhaps a child's tricycle in it; the balcony, a string of
colourful washing outside Milly's door; and the flat, in
which are Carol, Nick and Sal. The light is noticeably
brighter than it has been previously. The flat in particular
seems more spacious and airy, with no dark corners.*

Carol No. No problems at all really is there Nick.

,

I mean the garden makes a big difference. Nick's planted
her some bulbs, didn't you love.

Nick Cigarette?

Sal Thanks.

Nick lights their cigarettes.

(Thanks.)

Nick Damage your health.

Sal Sorry?

Nick Damage your health.

Sal Yes. Right you're right.

Sal faint laugh. Nick faint laugh.

Carol Nick's trying to stop, aren't you love.

Nick (*with a laugh*) (Fuck that.)

Sal faint laugh.

Carol I want him to try that hypnotist, don't I Nick.

Sal I've given up I'm afraid. (*She inhales.*)

'

I mean I've given up trying to give up.

Nick Right.

Sal If you see what I mean.

Nick Yeah well I've cut down haven't I Carol.

Sal faint laugh.
Sound of microwave timer. Carol heads for the kitchen.

Nick Hey. Carol.

Carol What?

Nick She doesn't believe I've cut down.

Sal and Carol both laugh. Carol goes out to the kitchen.

Because the thing is, well, it's addictive isn't it. Habit.

Sal and Nick fall silent, both smoking.

Sal Carol said –

Nick (*overlapping*) I'm trying to –

   Both faint laugh.

Nick (Sorry, I . . .) Yeah what were you saying.

Sal No you were –

Nick No no. You were saying something.

   '

Sal Carol said you were saying, I mean that sometimes you found Sharon, well, that she could be difficult sometimes.

Nick Yeah?

   '

No. No I wouldn't say that particularly.

   '

Sal Good.

Nick I mean I'm not saying she doesn't have her difficult moments. (I mean don't we all.)

   Silence. Carol comes in with food.

Carol (*to Sal*) You sure you don't want anything?

Sal I've just eaten thanks.

Carol Well if you change your mind. It's no trouble in the microwave. Nick treated me didn't you Nick.

   Nick sits to eat.

It's made a big difference. You know for her snacks and things.

Sal That's great.

Nick No waste, you know. (*He eats.*)

Sal (*brightly*) Well if I could just have a word with her now.

Carol What? Sharon? Yeah. Course. I mean well she's asleep at the moment isn't she Nick.

Nick (*with good humour*) Makes a change yeah.

Sal Well just a look at her then. If I could just take a look at her.

Carol Course.

    No one moves.

Nick. Nick she wants to have a look at her Nick. He's a bit slow sometimes aren't you love.

    Nick gets up, takes his chair, and places it in front of Sharon's door. They look expectantly at Sal.

Sal I'm sorry, I don't . . .

Nick What's that?

Sal I don't . . .

Carol Yeah you can see her. Through the glass. That's what we do, isn't it love, when she's asleep.

Nick (Makes a change yeah.)

Carol So it doesn't disturb her going in.

    ,

Sal Right. (*She doesn't move.*)

Nick You want a hand?

Sal Sorry?

Nick You want a hand up?

Sal No. Thanks. (It's alright thanks.)

    Sal gets onto the chair. She looks through the glass.

Carol She alright is she?

Sal Well actually . . . Look I can't . . .

Nick You're in your own light there.

  Sal moves her head. She peers through the glass.
  Silence.

Carol She alright?

Sal Fine. Yes. She looks fine. (What I can see . . .)

Carol Still right under is she.

Sal (*faint laugh*) Yes.

Carol Calls that doing a tortoise doesn't she Nick.

  All faint laugh. Sal makes to come down.

Nick Let me. (*He takes Sal's arm as she comes down.*)

Sal Thanks.

  He holds onto her arm a little too long.

(Thanks.)

Nick You're welcome. (*He puts the chair back and*
resumes eating.)

Carol Still needs a bit of a tidy in there.

Sal (*faint laugh*) Yes.

Carol You know what kids are like.

  Sal faint laugh. Nods.

Carol Got kids have you?

  '

Sal (No, no I haven't.) Look . . . If I could just go inside
for a moment. I'll be, I'll be very quiet.

Carol Course. Only it's probably locked at the moment that's the thing. She locks it you see, on the inside. Doesn't she Nick.

Sal (*lightly*) Why does she do that?

Nick (Funny kid yeah.)

Carol She just goes through phases doesn't she Nick. I mean I wish she wouldn't do it. Worries us when she does it actually.

Sal Couldn't you take away the key?

Carol That's right we're going to aren't we Nick. We're going to take it off her.

Sal I think you should.

,

Well. Look. I'll probably drop in again some time next week. Because naturally I would like to see –

Nick Sharon.

Sal Yes. Obviously I'd like to see her, and –

Carol Well that's fine. Any time. Just come along any time. Can't she Nick.

Nick gets up to see her out.

Sal Well I'm glad, I'm glad I've managed to meet –

Nick Nick.

Sal Yes. I'm glad I've managed to meet you Nick . . .

Nick Mutual.

Sal . . . at last.

Nick and Sal faint laugh.

174

(And that things seem to be . . .) Things are going well, yes?

All move towards the door.

Sal She's just had her birthday hasn't she.

Nick Yeah that's right.

Carol We had a little party for her actually, didn't we love.

Sal That was nice.

Carol Just us, you know.

Nick Cake. Candles.

,

Sal (*surprised and pleased*) That's nice. Good.

Nick Present

Sal Good that's very good.

They all smile.
Blackout.

PLAY WITH REPEATS

*If you go back now, everything
will be the same as before or worse . . .
You must understand that chances
are limited; no one has unlimited chances.
And you never know when you have used
your last chance.*

*Our misfortune is that we crawl about
like blind kittens on top of a table,
never knowing where the edge is.*

P. D. Ouspensky
Strange Life of Ivan Osokin

Play with Repeats was written under the Thames Television resident playwright scheme and first presented at the Orange Tree Theatre, Richmond, on 12 October 1989, with the following cast:

Anthony Steadman Thomas Wheatley
Nick/Terry Stephen Marchant
Kate/Franky Caroline Gruber
Mouhamed Lamine/Man in Launderette/Marc
  Ben Onwukwe
Mrs Dent/Man at Bus-Stop/Barbara Vivien Heilbron

Director Sam Walters
Designer Anne Gruenberg

Characters

Anthony Steadman
Nick/Terry
Kate/Franky
Mouhamed Lamine/Man in Launderette/Marc
Mrs Dent/Woman at Bus-Stop/Barbara

Time and Place

The place is London, but could be any city.
The time is best described as the present.
The locations are as follows:

ACT ONE

1. The Pub
2. At Lamine's
3.1. Custom Coils: The Workshop
3.2. Custom Coils: Franky's Office
4. A Temporary Bus-Stop

ACT TWO

1. A Launderette
2. The Pub
3. Custom Coils: The Workshop

Note

A pause is denoted throughout by a comma
on a separate line. It should no more be ignored
than a rest in a musical score may be ignored.

Act One

1. The Pub.

Tony is drinking with Nick, whose hair is distinctively cropped, dyed or gelled, and Kate, Nick's girlfriend. An electronic fruit-machine is faintly audible in the silences.

Nick You want to ask me a question.

Tony Yes. What is there that you regret?

Nick What?

Tony What do you regret?

'

Nick Nothing.

Tony What d'you mean nothing?

Nick I mean nothing.

Kate and Nick exchange a faint laugh.

Tony No, listen: I'm talking about the things you've done in your life.

Nick Right. So what's wrong with your life?

Tony No I'm not asking you . . .

Nick I know that.

Tony . . . to tell me, to tell me what's wrong with my life.

Nick I know that.

'

So let's leave it.

Tony What I'm asking you is if you've ever regretted anything. Yourself as a person.

Nick As a person.

Tony Because I'm not asking you to tell me what's wrong with my life. Because alright I know what's wrong with it. I have insight into that.

Nick Uh-huh.

,

You're taking it too seriously.

Tony What?

Nick You're taking it –

Tony My life. I'm taking it too seriously.

Nick You've put your finger on it.

Tony Well thank you very much.

,

Nick There you are.

Tony Thank you very much.

Nick There you are. Look at yourself. You're taking it too seriously.

Tony Well thank you. Fuck you as a matter of fact.

Nick That's fine.

Tony Fuck you.

,

Nick My pleasure.

Tony Because whoever you are . . .

Kate All the world's a stage.

Tony . . . you're not in a position to pass judgement.

Nick Really.

Kate We're actors. The world's a stage.

Tony I'm sorry, but that's a meaningless remark.

Nick She's right.

Kate We strut. We fret.

Nick She's right.

Tony No, I'm sorry but she isn't right. How can that be right? I mean this isn't an act. This is me. I'm here. I'm making decisions. I could've stayed over there where I normally sit but no I've come over here of my own free will to speak to you both because I have something to say. An actor is repeating a part, but this is different, this is entirely different.

,

This is significant. This is me.

Kate It's a tale told by an idiot.

Tony Is that supposed to be a comment?

Kate Signifying nothing.

Tony Is that supposed to be some kind of a comment?

,

Well is it?

Nick Leave it.

Kate It's actually poetry.

Nick Let's leave it.

Tony Poetry.

Nick This is an actress. You're talking to an actress.

,

Tony What's that – a professional actress?

Kate I'm Kate. Yes.

Tony I'm sorry. Hello Kate.

Kate Hello.

Tony Anthony. And I apologise. Because I respect your profession.

Kate Thank you.

Tony But as an actress – whatever kind of actress you are – I know that you'll have insight into human nature.

Nick I'll tell you what I do regret.

,

Tony Because that's your job.

Nick I'll tell you what I do regret.

Tony I'd like you to.

Nick What I regret, my friend, is the fact that you exist.

Kate laughs and puts her arm around Nick.

Kate He doesn't mean that.

Tony No that's absolutely fine by me. Because I take that –

Nick Don't I?

Tony I take that in the spirit in which it was intended.

Nick No offence.

Tony That is to say i.e. as an example. A trivial example.
Absolutely. None taken.

*Nick and Kate kiss. Tony continues as if he had their
attention.*

Because no one's denying, Kate, that we learn from our
mistakes. And I accept your point that a poet can turn
that into poetry. That's fine. But for the rest of us who
are not poets which is the vast majority, by the time
we've learned from our mistakes it's already too late.
Those opportunities will never return. And even if you
study life, even if you write books about it, you can still
find yourself in the launderette, not to do your washing,
I mean just to keep *warm*.

Kate slips away.

Where's she going?

Nick What d'you mean?

Tony Katy. Where's Katy going?

Nick She's going to the toilet.

Tony OK. Fine.

Nick She's just going to the toilet.

Tony No, that's fine.

,

Listen –

Nick You have something against that?

Tony No. Listen. How old am I?

Nick (*shrugs*) Forty?

Tony How did you know that?

,

That's exactly right. I'm thirty-nine, and tomorrow I'll be forty.

Nick Crisis in other words.

Tony No, are you psychic?

Nick Congratulations.

Tony What? No. Not congratulations.

Nick OK.

Tony Not congratulations, because . . .

,

Because. Alright?

Nick Because.

Tony Because I will be forty years old tomorrow, and over those forty years, what have I accumulated?

Nick (*shrugs*) Money?

Tony Money, no.

,

No I'm not speaking in a material sense.

Nick Give up.

Tony Wisdom.

Nick Wisdom.

Tony Yes, we accumulate wisdom, but what use is it to us? Because the events when the wisdom would've been useful, they're over and gone.

Nick Well then that's how it is.

Tony No that's *not* how it is.

Nick Well then I'm sorry, I don't understand what you're saying.

Tony That's alright.

,

No that's alright. I accept that because what I'm trying to say is not rational.

Nick It's not rational.

Tony No.

,

Nick Fine.

Tony I mean how old are you?

,

Nick Why? Twenty-eight.

Tony And what's your profession?

Nick My profession?

Tony Yes, what do you do?

Nick Do I have a job?

Tony Yes.

Nick (*faint laugh*) No.

Tony In other words you missed the opportunity. The opportunity was there, but at the crucial moment you said to yourself: this isn't me.

Nick What opportunity?

Tony To work. To get a job. Because if that opportunity presented itself again – and what I'm suggesting to you is that that could be possible – you wouldn't say: this isn't me. You'd seize it. You wouldn't be coming here . . .

Nick I happen to like coming here . . .

Tony Night after night.

Nick I like coming here.

Tony You like coming here.

,

Don't deceive yourself.

Kate returns.

Don't deceive yourself. You and Katy here make an attractive couple, as I was saying. But why does an attractive couple come in here night after night to drink this stuff and sit in basically silence?

,

Nick It's Anthony's birthday.

Kate Congratulations Anthony.

Tony Tomorrow. Thank you.

Kate Are you doing anything?

Tony Tomorrow? Not doing as such. No.

As Tony drains his glass, Kate whispers to Nick.

Nick (*prompted by Kate*) Look, d'you want another drink, Tone?

Tony Sorry?

Nick Your birthday. You want a – ?

Kate Well of course he does.

Tony A drink? Well yes, if you're . . .

Nick Pils?

Tony Holsten Pils. Thank you very much.

Nick This dead?

Tony Thanks. Thanks a lot.

Nick goes with the empties. Silence punctuated by faint fruit machine.

Fantastic. You look fantastic.

Kate faint laugh.

Tony You have a lovely face.

Kate Thank you.

Tony Have I said that before?

Kate No.

Tony Because I know I have a habit, I know I've a habit of repeating myself.

Kate You didn't say that before.

Tony Good, that's, good. You have a lovely face.

Kate Thank you.

Tony You have a lovely face, but you've still failed. Why is that?

Kate (*faint laugh*) I haven't failed.

Tony Of course you've failed. Look.

Kate What?

Tony It's there in your eyes.

,

Kate Listen, I –

Tony I didn't want to say that but it's there in your eyes, Kate. What does an actress do in the evenings? An actress works. She's known. I mean Kate what? Kate who? If you weren't here what difference would it make to anything? And naturally you persuade yourself that there is an intention, that it's meant to be like this, it's meant to be. But what does meant to be mean? Meant to be doing the same thing for eighteen years? Meant to be keeping warm next to a clothes-drier while someone writes reports? No way.

,

No way, Kate. Meant to be means nothing.

Kate What reports?

Tony Because listen, what are we, you and I?

Kate Wait a minute, wait a minute. Don't include me in this.

Tony We're human beings.

Kate Don't include me.

Tony We're human beings. And perhaps I'm repeating myself, but for human beings everything should be possible. The language we speak tells us that. It tells us that the potential – by which I mean not only what we could be, but what we might've been – the potential is infinite. And so what's *meant* to happen – which is surely the realisation of that potential – are you with me? – what's meant to happen, hasn't happened. And what *has* happened – what's happened to us – was not meant to happen. No.

,

How can we believe that about ourselves? Because listen –

Kate I'm listening.

Tony OK.

,

Yes?

Kate I'm listening to you.

Tony Good.

Kate No, I'm interested.

Tony Well you should be.

Kate I am. What are you suggesting?

Tony That's good. Because listen, I normally sit over there and every night I see you, the two of you, over here, and don't you understand my heart bleeds.

Kate And if I happen to like it here?

Tony It bleeds for you. What d'you mean: like it here? That's exactly what *he* said. (*Picks up a bottle.*) Don't you know what this stuff is doing to your body? If you got pregnant? What sort of baby you might have?

Kate (*betraying sadness*) That's unlikely.

Tony Exactly.

,

Yes, exactly.

Kate So what are you suggesting?

Tony (*intensely*) What I'm suggesting, Kate, is that there is a train. It's going into the tunnel. The children are waving.

,

I'm suggesting that if we could only go *back*.

,

Kate faint laugh – but the idea is attractive.

Tony Yes.

Kate You can't go back.

Tony Yes, but if only we could. Live our lives again. Knowing what we do now. Knowing that. Don't you see?

As Nick approaches with new bottles, Tony takes a card from his pocket and passes it to Kate.

Kate What's this?

Tony Look at it. Read it.

Kate 'Mouhamed Lamine . . .'

Tony Mouhamed Lamine. Read it.

Nick Pils.

Tony Cheers.

Kate 'Mouhamed Lamine . . .'

Nick What?

Kate '. . . African . . .' What's that?

Tony Marabout.

Kate 'African Marabout. Psychologist, telepathist, clairvoyant . . .'

Nick Let's have a look.

Kate I'm reading. 'Treats all physical and psychological problems. Assures success in business, marriage and competitive sports. Counteracts evil influences . . .'

Tony Go on.

Kate 'Action at a distance. Can overcome any problem even if it seems impossible. Results guaranteed. Please bring . . .' What?

Tony Ring. It's a misprint. Please ring.

Kate 'Please ring this number any time.'

Tony That's right.

Kate and Nick examine the card.

Can I have the card please.

Nick I'm reading.

,

Tony You see: even if it seems impossible.

Kate So what's 'action at a distance'?

Tony Spoons, bending spoons. But that's just an example of what can be achieved. Marabout. That means Holy Man.

Nick Where d'you get this?

Tony Launderette. I was given it. (*He pours some beer. His hand is shaking.*) I just went in there to dry some shirts, and I was given it.

Kate He wants to go back.

Nick What, to the launderette?

Kate laughs.

Tony A man like this, he doesn't inhabit the world in a material sense. Meaning he can see.

Nick See what?

Kate That everything is possible.

Nick Oh. Right.

Nick and Kate exchange a glance.

Of course.

Tony What, you think I wouldn't?

Nick Wouldn't what?

Tony You think I'm weak? Because I'm not weak.

Kate Wouldn't what?

Tony What?

Kate Wouldn't do what?

Tony Wouldn't ring him. Because I would. I intend to.

Nick Mr Lamine.

Tony Yes. Because I'm not afraid.

Kate Afraid of what? What's he afraid of?

Tony I'm not afraid.

Nick I don't know. What *are* you afraid of?

Tony I'm not.

Nick Right. So that's OK.

Tony That's what I'm saying.

Nick Absolutely.

Tony Because there's a limit.

Nick Well absolutely. You've reached it. You've reached your limit.

Tony Will you give me the card please.

Nick One moment.

Nick produces a plastic teaspoon. He holds it out with ceremony in both hands.

Observe.

He slowly bends the spoon. It snaps. Kate laughs.

Tony I don't understand.

Nick I'm just making a point. (*Ignoring Tony, he begins to walk away.*)

Tony I'd like my card. Don't just walk away from me!

Tony seizes Nick who turns and produces a knife.

You know what you're doing.

Nick You tell me.

Tony You're drinking yourself to death . . .

Nick Am I.

Tony . . . in here.

,

Nick Something so trivial.

Nick drops the card and goes to play the fruit machine. Tony retrieves it.

Tony What's wrong with him?

Kate Nick? That's just what he's like. So, you're going to ring your friend?

Tony Who's that?

Kate Lamine, Mouhamed Lamine. (*faint laugh*)

Tony Why not?

Kate Why not?

Tony goes to the phone, inserts money and punches
the number. His side of the phone-call may form a
kind of antiphony with the electronic tunes of the fruit
machine.

Tony Mr Lamine? – Ah. OK. (*to Kate*) He's coming. Mr
Lamine? – Yes, hello, I'm . . . What it is is I've got one
of your cards here and I was wondering . . . – That's
right. – That's exactly right. – Well whenever you . . . –
No, I work during the day. – Yes, an evening, an evening
would be fine. – Now? – Well yes, I suppose, yes I could. –
Yes. Thank you. – Yes I have. – It's here on the card. –
No. Fine. That's absolutely fine. – Fifteen minutes.
Fourth landing. I've got it. – I'm sorry? – Right. Yes.
I look forward to it. (*Hangs up.*) He knew my name.

Kate What?

Tony He knew my name: he said I'll see you in fifteen
minutes, Mr Steadman.

Kate Mr what?

Tony That's my name . . .

Kate You gave him your name.

Tony Steadman.

Kate Come on. You *gave* him your name. I heard you.

She goes and puts her arms around Nick, turning back
to Tony

You're drunk. Go home.

Tony He knew my name.

The fruit machine spits out money.
Blackout.

2. At Lamine's.

Lamine's room. Subdued light. Tony is alone for a few moments, then Mrs Dent enters. In silence she fastens a piece of string to a hook in the wall and attaches the other end to the back of a chair. The string bisects the stage. She turns to Tony.

Mrs Dent Mr Lamine will be with you shortly. Please don't touch the string.

> *Mrs Dent goes. Tony contemplates the string.*
> *Lamine enters. Black, blind, and perhaps wearing an anorak, he is not obviously mysterious. He gropes for the string and feels his way along it to the chair before Tony speaks.*

Tony You knew my name.

Lamine I'm sorry?

Tony How did you do that?

'

This isn't what I expected.

Lamine That's in the nature of things.

Tony Right. (*faint laugh*)

'

No. Right. I know exactly what you mean.

Lamine One day we realise we've spent our lives dreaming. But waking up is difficult.

Tony I can see that.

Lamine You can?

'

My rate is a pound a minute. I take it you have cash.

Tony Well I've got –

Lamine Fifteen minutes is fifteen pounds, thirty minutes will be thirty. And so on.

Tony I see.

Lamine After sixty minutes that is to say i.e. one hour, subsequent minutes are half that rate but the minimum unit of charge is then ten minutes or in other words five pounds.

Tony Right.

Lamine You follow.

Tony You don't think it seems rather –

Lamine I'm joking.

'

Tony I'm sorry?

Lamine I'm joking. I'm not serious. Let me tell you about the idiot who comes to the city. One day an idiot comes to the city for the very first time. He's never seen so many people before, such enormous crowds in constant movement. That night, when his money runs out, he makes his way to Waterloo and finds a broken box to sleep in. But he's afraid that when he wakes up, he won't recognise himself among so many other people. So what the idiot does is he finds a scrap of chalk and makes a mark on the box.

Tony Chalk.

Lamine The mark you see is so that he can identify himself when he wakes up. (*Faint laugh which Tony joins in.*) But. But in the night, someone steals the broken box, and crawls into it. So in the morning the idiot wakes up on the ground and the first thing he sees is this man in the box with the chalk mark on it. And he goes up to the other man and he says: well it's perfectly clear who *you* are – but in that case, who the fuck am *I*?

Big laugh from Lamine. Tony joins in uncertainly.

Tony Right.

Lamine Who the fuck am I.

Tony No, that's very good.

,

Lamine One day we realise we've spent our lives dreaming, but you can wake up in different ways.

Tony That's what I want to do.

Lamine You want to wake up.

Tony Yes.

Lamine You want to wake up, but at some point in the past.

Tony Yes. How did you know that?

Lamine And why not? If we can imagine it, why shouldn't it be possible?

Tony That's right. That's basically what I've been saying all evening. But these people, all they can do is trivialise. I mean, why a man has to do that to his hair . . .

Lamine I know.

Tony They're so limited. Just because *they've* failed . . .

Lamine I know, I know.

Tony So he takes out a knife. Any fool can take out a knife.

Lamine I know.

In silence Lamine feels his way along the string to Tony. He raises his hand.

She's coming.

Tony Who?

Lamine Remind me to tell you the one about death.

Tony Who's coming?

Lamine We both need a drink.

Mrs Dent enters.

Lamine Two Stellas.

Mrs Dent goes. Lamine makes his way back along the string during the following:

Tony What I've come to see is that my life –

Lamine You're happy with Stella?

Tony Stella.

Lamine Stella Artois. The Carlsberg I'm afraid is finished.

Tony What, Special Brews.

Lamine The Carlsberg Special Brews. They're finished.

Tony I'm a Pils man.

Lamine Holsten Pils.

Tony Holsten Pils . . . Lowenbrau . . .

Lamine I'm sorry we can't offer you a choice.

Tony I'm happy with Stella.

Lamine (*raises hand*) She's coming.

'

Tony No actually I'm surprised. I thought someone in your position would have to –

Lamine My position.

Tony Yes, would have to abstain.

Lamine Abstain?

Tony Yes.

Lamine No. No, that's not necessary.

Mrs Dent enters with beer.

Mr Steadman would like me to abstain.

Mrs Dent laughs softly.

Mrs Dent is my eyes, aren't you, Mrs Dent. She is my eyes, and at times, my feet.

Mrs Dent I told him not to touch the string.

Lamine I don't think he would touch the string.

Lamine and Tony open cans. Mrs Dent lingers.

Mrs Dent Mr Lamine, there are some people –

Lamine Tell them to go away.

Mrs Dent It's that woman –

Lamine I know.

Mrs Dent It's that woman who lost her baby.

Lamine I know, I know. Tell her to go away.

Mrs Dent goes.

I'm sorry. There are some things I'm not prepared to do.

They drink.

Tony I feel very –

Lamine (*overlapping*) People think –

Tony Sorry.

Lamine No. Go on.

Tony You were –

Lamine No. Please go on.

'

Tony I wanted to –

Lamine (*overlapping*) Please –

Tony What?

Lamine Please go on.

Tony I wanted to say –

Lamine You must go on.

Tony Yes, to say . . . just to say: I feel very . . . relaxed here. It isn't what I imagined.

Lamine Relaxed.

Tony Yes.

Lamine Good.

'

Good. Is that all?

Tony No. Well no. Obviously . . . (*decisive*) Two things.

Lamine Good.

Tony The first . . .
   Well look I have a particular way of folding my shirts . . .
   No, let me go back a bit.
   What I'm trying to say is, is I live on my own as it were, which is fine, which is absolutely fine, as far as

it goes. I mean it's something that I have insight into.
Because it's something that's happened largely out of
choice. And I mean the room itself limits, largely limits
what I do, because of its size. Because if I were to invite
somebody back – let's say from the pub – then it would
be embarrassing, the size of the room being such that . . .
you would be too close to the other person at any given
time. They would question your motives. So in a sense
the room itself imposes certain limits, which I accept.
It's certainly very convenient for me. Just a bus-ride from
my job. And I have a range of appliances. And the toilet
is a reasonable distance. I mean it's not so close that you
hear everyone else, but it's not so far away that you have
to make other arrangements, d'you see what I mean. The
microwave has made a big difference, naturally. It means
you're completely your own master when it comes to
meals. You can have a hot meal any time although in
practice I tend to eat at quarter past six and maybe a
little earlier at weekends. So what I'm saying is, is I have
insight into that. I can see myself folding my shirts and
I realise I do it in a particular way which I'd be loath to
change. But then I met Heather, and –

Lamine Who is . . .

Tony Heather? Right. Yes. Sorry.

Lamine Don't be.

Tony No. I'm sorry.

Lamine Don't be.

,

Heather.

Tony Yes. Heather is . . . No, this is the whole point.
Because some time ago, Heather and I . . . I met Heather.

And with Heather. You see this is something I've never been able to do before, to initiate a relationship –

Lamine This is a physical relationship.

Tony Physical. Yes. Certainly physical. But more than that. Undoubtedly physical, but more than that it's . . . Yes, exactly what you were saying. It's like waking up, but when you look out of the window, instead of the Complex . . .

Lamine Which is . . .

Tony There's a Leisure Complex at the back of us and we're always in its shadow. But instead of that it's as if there's a landscape . . .

Lamine Opening up.

Tony Yes. How did you know that? It's opening up. That's right. And what I saw was the possibility of another life. Not this. Not this life. But the possibility . . . I don't know . . . of love . . . an act of love . . . starting a family . . . not this life.

,

But you see – and of course I know this now – what I did – and I did this in good faith – but what I did was, which is what I regret, was I failed to assert myself. Because in respecting her – which I do, which I still do – as a person, I realise now I didn't give her the necessary attention as a woman. I didn't assert myself as a man.

Lamine She was afraid of you.

Tony That's right.

,

That's exactly right. Terrified. How did you know?

Lamine And this went on for how long?

Tony Sorry?

,

No, we met once. Only this once. Just by chance. At a bus-stop

Lamine A bus-stop.

Tony A temporary bus-stop

Lamine And the second?

Tony I'm sorry?

Lamine There were two things.

Tony Of course, yes. I . . .

Lamine (*raises hand*) She's coming.

,

Tony What, shall I . . .

Lamine No. Please go on.

Tony No, the other thing is my job.

Mrs Dent enters softly during the following and picks up the ring-pulls.

Because alright, I've been doing the same thing – which is winding coils – for eighteen years now. Yes. Eighteen years. I wind coils for loudspeakers, quality loudspeakers, which in itself is not something I regret. On the contrary I have the satisfaction – which is why I've never gone in for office work – the satisfaction of possessing a skill, and knowing that because of that skill I've made myself indispensable, i.e. this is something that not many people can say about themselves. Whereas the others – Terry for example – is not what you'd call skilled and he makes a lot of sexual remarks which I would find offensive as a woman. But what I'm getting at *is*, is you would've thought – and correct me if I'm wrong – but you would've thought that someone with eighteen years experience . . . Because when Barry left with his heart they needed a new Supervisor, and the essential thing here is that I wasn't even told the job was *advertised*. No. By the time I found that out – which in itself was purely a matter of chance – they'd already appointed someone else – Marc – who happens to be black – which I only mention – because we get on very well – but the fact remains that his previous place of employment was a Pizza Hut.

What I should've done – and of course I see this now so clearly – is the moment Barry left, I shouldn't've waited, I should've gone to personnel, I should've spoken to Franky, who is an intelligent girl, and I should've seized that opportunity. After all it's not as if I'm frightened of Franky, (*faint laugh*) who is in fact younger than myself. It's not as if I don't have every reason to go in there and ask her for what is mine by rights. Surely.

'

It's not fear. It's . . .

'

You see this is something I was destined to do.

Mrs Dent That's an odd choice of words.

Tony Look, I'm sorry, does she have to –

Lamine Mrs Dent is my eyes.

Mrs Dent It's just a comment.

Tony I'm not asking for comments.

'

I'm not asking for comments. I mean what exactly is her role in this?

Mrs Dent Mouhamed found my husband. He'd gone off and taken the children. What he'd done was he'd locked them in a room. (*She takes Lamine's hand. She begins to weep.*) Mouhamed saw the room. He could see them in the room. He could describe them. He could describe their faces.

Lamine comforts her. Excluded by this private grief. Tony finally speaks to draw attention to himself.

Tony I'm not asking for comments.

Lamine You're asking to go back.

Tony Yes. Knowing what I do now.

Lamine And this is what you want.

Tony It's what I came here for.

Lamine If that's what you want, no problem.

Tony No problem.

Lamine No problem.

,

If that's what you want.

Tony You keep saying that.

Lamine Well – OK.

,

Tony So, what, there's some kind of . . . procedure?

Lamine Procedure?

Mrs Dent There is no procedure.

,

Tony Right. Meaning . . .

Lamine That's it.

Tony Meaning that's it. OK.

,

Lamine OK?

Tony Thank you.

Lamine Provided of course you believe that it's possible.

Tony I wouldn't be here, Mr Lamine –

Lamine Because there are some people – aren't there – they ask me to bend a spoon and I bend a spoon. But they look at the spoon and they say: this spoon is straight.

Tony No, that's exactly right. I understand that mentality.

Lamine This spoon is straight.

Tony The pub where I drink, that's exactly the mentality.

Lamine Christ could appear in the garden.

Tony This spoon is straight. That's just what they'd say.

Lamine He could appear in the garden and exhibit his wounds.

Tony Well that's right.

Lamine Jesus Christ could appear.

Tony I know. That's exactly –

Lamine (*very lightly*) Let me tell you the one about death.

,

A man is queueing up in a cafeteria at Kings Cross Station when he notices death a little way ahead of him, paying for a ham and salad sandwich. Overwhelmed by panic he slips out of the queue, replaces his tray, withdraws all his money from the bank and flies immediately to a Greek island. Later in the day death happens to be chatting to one of the man's friends in the Farringdon Road. Where is so-and-so these days, says death. Oh, says the friend, he'll be hanging round a station or sitting in a pub somewhere. He's a bit cautious and he never goes far. Well that's what I thought, says death, but the thing is, is he's down here on my list, and in a couple of days' time I'm due to collect him from Corfu of all places. (*He laughs.*) Corfu of all places.

Lamine continues to laugh, joined by Mrs Dent, who has been winding up the string during the latter part of this story. Tony also laughs, uncertainly.

Tony No. Corfu. That's very good.

Blackout.

3.1. Custom Coils: The Workshop.

Harsh light. Loud music. Tony and Terry are working. They both wear a kind of surgical hat whose function is more symbolic than practical. Tony has his back to the room, and in addition to the hat he wears ear-cans to block out the noise of the radio. Nothing for some time except light and noise. Then Franky, the personnel manager, enters. She crosses the room to collect some documents, unnoticed by Tony, but immediately attracting Terry's attention. Only fragments of the following are audible.

Terry Looks to me like someone was up last night.
   Tell him he can put one in for me next time.
   If you're not getting the satisfaction you need love, just let me know. Satisfaction's my middle name.

If you like music come round some time and have a go on my equipment.
You just let me know.
First the mashed potatoes, then the gravy.

Oblivious to this, Franky goes out with the documents.

Terry Hey Tony. FIRE! FIRE! EARTHQUAKE! END OF THE FUCKING WORLD!

Terry laughs. Tony of course hears none of this, but as if sensing something he turns round slowly and discovers Terry laughing. Tony also laughs, uncertainly, attempting to share the joke, before turning back to his work.

(*unvoiced, without rancour*) Fucking idiot.

Franky enters again. The music persists.

Franky Mr Steadman. Mr Steadman.

No response from Tony. Terry laughs, shakes his head.

Mr Steadman.
Will you turn that off, Terry. Turn it off. Now.

Terry laughs, pretends not to understand, but complies. Silence.

Mr Steadman.

Terry If you want his attention Franky love, you'll have to put your hand down his trousers.

Franky Will you shut up.

Terry On second thoughts, put it down mine and I'll pass on the message.

Franky looks at him.

Joke, Franky.

,

Joke.

Tony, sensing something, turns and sees Franky. He removes the ear-cans.

Franky Mr Steadman.

Tony Yes. Sorry. Have you been trying to –

Franky There was a note. There was a note saying you wanted to see me.

Terry Go for it Tony.

Tony What?

Terry Joke.

,

Joke.

Tony That's right. If it's convenient.

Franky Fine.

She waits.

Tony No, it's just that . . .

Franky No, that's fine. I understand. Let's say in my office in two minutes, shall we.

Tony Right. Thanks.

Terry Steady on, Tony.

Tony Two minutes then.

Franky Fine.

Terry You don't know what forces you're unleashing there, my love. I mean what we're basically talking about here is a man who gets a hard-on when he touches your coffee cup.

Tony Hey, leave it out.

Terry Which he does frequently.

> *Franky has gone. Both men faint laugh. Tony is embarrassed but flattered by this reference to his 'virility'. Silence.*

So you want Barry's job?

Tony What?

Terry I said you want –

Tony That's right.

Terry Barry's job.

,

She won't give you that.

Tony Uh-huh. She won't.

Terry She won't give you Barry's job.

Tony Well we'll see.

,

Won't we. We'll see about that.

Terry And I'll tell you why.

,

I'll tell you why.

Tony What d'you know about it?

Terry I'll tell you why.

Tony Because in point of fact you don't know what you're talking about.

Terry Don't I.

Tony Well you tell me.

Terry Don't I, mate.

Tony You tell me then.

,

You tell me why.

Terry I'll tell you why.

Tony Fine that's fine. Do so.

Terry I'll tell you why, and the reason is she's frigid.

,

Exactly.

Tony Come on . . .

Terry She is basically frigid. You could go in that office. You could give her mashed potatoes and gravy. And you still wouldn't get Barry's job. And d'you know why?

Tony (*gets out a newspaper cutting*) You see, look at this.

Terry D'you know why: because she would feel nothing. Butter wouldn't melt, mate.

Tony No, look at this.

Terry So what's this? (*He turns the paper in his hand, affecting indifference.*)

Tony Well you can see what it is.

Terry I know what it *is*.

,

I mean I don't need you to tell me what it *is*.

Tony So this time I'm going to ask for an explanation.

Terry (*passing back the paper*) Yeah, you should.

Tony You think?

Terry Something like that, you definitely should.

,

That Christmas party I could've had her.

Tony Had who?

,

Terry He asks who.

Tony (*faint laugh*) Franky?

Terry He asks who. Of course Franky.

Tony But weren't you . . . I thought you were –

Terry I could've had her. Don't tell me I couldn't.

Tony OK.

Terry Don't tell me I couldn't alright. Because the fuck –

Tony OK.

Terry The fuck you know about it.

,

Which is how I know.

,

Tony How you know what?

Terry How I know. Because she was up against that wall. She was up against that boardroom wall, and believe me she wanted it.

Tony Alright.

Terry Whatever she *says*.

,

Tony What does she say?

Terry She doesn't *say* anything. She wouldn't, would she. But she doesn't have to. Because she knows. And she knows that next time it will be different.

Tony Uh-huh.

Terry Whatever she *says*.

They fall silent. Terry produces a gift-wrapped bottle and tosses it to Tony.

Tony What's this?

Terry Happy returns, that's all.

Tony (*moved*) Thanks. Thanks a lot.

Terry We do what we can.

Tony No. Really. How did you know?

Terry Barbara knew.

Tony Did she? So is she coming in?

Terry No, she phoned. She can't.

,

Tony A gift. This has never happened before.

Franky enters.

Franky If you'd like to come in now.

Tony stands, removes hat.

Tony Right. (*to Terry.*) Thank you very much.

Terry Put one in for me, Tony.

Blackout.

217

3.2. Custom Coils: Franky's Office.

Tony nurses the present. Silence. Franky is not of course the cold stereotype of Terry's imagining. Throughout what follows her concern is to do what's best for Tony.

Tony Listen, I'm sorry about –

Franky Don't worry about Terry. If this organisation was slightly larger we'd be *obliged* to employ a certain number of mentally handicapped people.

   Both faint laugh.

Today's your birthday.

Tony That's right.

Franky Congratulations.

Tony Thank you.

Franky Are you doing anything?

Tony Sorry? No. No I'm not.

   ,

Not doing as such.

Franky What did you want to see me about?

Tony Right. OK. Yes. (*decisive*) Two things.

Franky Two things. Fine.

Tony Yuh. No. What am I saying? One.

Franky One thing. That's fine.

Tony I'm not making myself –

Franky You are. Perfectly clear.

Tony Am I?

Franky Perfectly.

Tony Right.

,

Tony Right, the thing is – this is what's confusing – is last time this happened –

Franky Last time what happened?

Tony Ah. No. You wouldn't – of course you wouldn't – you wouldn't be aware of that.

Franky I'm not.

Tony No.

   Both faint laugh.

No. Forget that.

Franky Fine.

Tony I digress. (*faint laugh*)

Franky No that's fine. What did you want to see me about?

Tony (*intensely*) I want Barry's job. Barry's left. I want his job.

Franky Uh-huh . . .

Tony That's it. I want his job.

,

Franky This is the . . .

Tony The supervising job, that's right. (*He takes out the newspaper cutting.*) Because look: this is . . .
   What I'm trying to say is, is I only came across this by chance, Franky – Miss Wood – by chance –

Franky Franky's fine.

Tony Purely by chance. Purely by chance I come across an advertisement for this job – because no one has approached me – I find an advertisement for something which is by rights mine. And all I'm trying to say is, is how would *you* feel, is why wasn't my attention directed to this?

Franky Listen, we're obliged to advertise.

Tony I realise you're obliged. I accept that. But why wasn't I approached? Because everybody knows that when you do that – when you advertise – that's just to cover yourself – so you cover yourself – and then you appoint your man from the inside.

Franky Not necessarily.

Tony No.

,

No. Agreed. Not necessarily, but this is my job.

Franky You can certainly apply.

Tony Something that is mine by rights.

Franky You can apply.

Tony You keep saying that. You keep saying that: apply. But no way am I going to compete.

,

No way. Because I can compete and I know what will happen: what will happen is what happened before.

Franky Before what?

Tony And it won't happen again.

,

Franky Before what?

Tony Something I'm quite clearly destined to do.

Franky That's an odd choice of words.

Tony Well I'm sorry.

Franky In the context. I just mean in what amounts to a fairly trivial context.

Tony Well I'm sorry about the context, but the context is my life.

Franky That's not what I meant.

Tony And I'm sorry if it happens to be trivial.

Franky That's not what I meant.

The phone rings.

Look, I didn't realise you'd feel so strongly about this.

Tony Well I do, Miss Wood. I feel very strongly.

Franky D'you mind if I take this call.

She answers the phone.

Custom Coils. Frances Wood speaking. – Right, will you tell him I'm in a meeting. – I should think about two more minutes. – OK. Thanks.

She hangs up. Silence.

No one is questioning your skill, Tony.

Tony Good. Thank you.

Franky But this isn't the same kind of job. This is about managing people.

Tony Right. Human nature.

,

Human nature, I have insight into that.

Franky Fine, that's fine. Barbara in today?

Tony No. Apparently she phoned.

Franky What, she's depressed?

Tony I should think so. She usually is.

Franky She has to be watched.

Tony (*faint laugh*) That time she cut her wrists . . .

Franky Which time are we talking about?

Tony The third time: the third time when she cut them at home and then came into work on the bus. (*faint laugh*) That's a half-hour journey. Only Barbara could do that.

Franky I know.

Tony Well it's a cry for help of course. It's not actually serious. It's just that particular time, the blood . . .

Franky She has to be watched.

Tony That's right. And the tears. Every day there are tears . . .

Franky She'll destroy things to get your attention.

Tony Well that's right.

Franky There's Terry . . .

,

Tony Destroy things. No, you're absolutely right about her.

Franky There's Terry. Now you probably realise what Terry wants . . .

Tony I know. It must be embarrassing for you. No, if I was responsible I'd put a stop to that. You see it's ever since the Christmas party . . .

Franky The Christmas party.

'

What d'you mean, the Christmas party?

Tony Well ever since –

Franky Ever since what? I'm not talking about his imagination. I'm talking about the fact that what he needs, is someone to permanently hold his hand.

Tony (*nods*) Hold his hand, right.

Franky Hold his hand. Because you must know for example that Terry can't read or write.

'

You do know that?

Tony Uh-huh.

'

Read or write. But he seems to –

Franky Yes he manages . . .

Tony Because he seems to manage . . .

Franky Yes he manages, but the reason he manages, is because Barry's always helped him. Barry explains the orders. Barry fills in his time-sheet. He brings in a paper and tells Terry what's going to be on television. Sometimes he writes letters for him. This is quite apart from his actual *work*.

Tony Uh-huh.

Franky OK? I just want to make sure you realise what can be involved.

The phone's ringing.

223

Tony It just makes you wonder –

Franky D'you mind if I take this.

She answers the phone.

Custom Coils. Frances Wood speaking. – Yes. OK. I'm still in a meeting. – Tell him I'll be with him in one minute. – OK. Thanks. (*She hangs up.*)

Tony It makes you wonder why you employ people like that.

Faint laugh from Franky. She lights a cigarette. Silence.

Franky Look, you can have the job.

Tony Yuh?

,

No. I'm amazed.

Franky If that's what you want.

Tony It's what I came in here for, Miss Wood.

Franky Franky.

Tony Franky.

Franky Well – OK.

Tony I'm amazed.

Franky Don't be amazed.

Tony I am. I'm amazed.

Franky If that's what you want.

Tony (*laughing*) Thank you.

Franky (*laughing*) Don't thank me.

Tony No. Thank you.

Franky Because obviously you feel strongly, and if that's
what you want . . .

Tony You keep saying that.

Franky . . . then it's yours.

Tony You keep saying that.

,

Because –

Franky No, that's fine.

Tony I'm amazed.

Franky It's a good opportunity for you.

Tony Well that's right.

,

It is. And I knew that this time if I just . . . put myself
forward, asserted myself. If I actually came to you –

Franky Well you have. I'm very pleased.

Tony Because I'm thinking of starting a family.

Franky Well I'm very pleased for you.

,

Now look . . .

Tony I don't believe this.

Franky Look, I can't immediately put my hands on the
details . . .

Tony That's not a problem.

Franky Obviously the conditions of service will be
exactly the same . . .

Tony Right.

Franky No union membership.

Tony Right. Yes.

Franky After two more years continuous service, there'll be another day's annual holiday.

Tony Right.

Franky Obviously you'll be on the next pay increment.

Tony Right. Good.

Franky We'll have to advertise your present job obvi –

Tony Obviously. Right.

Franky And you will need to apply in writing for this one.

Tony Formality. I understand that.

Franky (*terminating interview*) Right.

Tony That's it.

Franky That's it.

Tony There's no . . .

Franky What?

Tony There's no . . .

Franky Probationary period? Absolutely not. No, we'll just put you straight in at that grade.

Tony OK.

Franky OK?

The phone's ringing.

Fine. I must . . .

Tony I'll see myself out.

Franky answers the phone. Tony heads for the door, but turns back and waits in the room.

Franky Custom Coils. Frances Wood. – Yes, put him
through. – Geoffrey, yes, I'm sorry. – I know. – Yes I
know. We're going to have to change that procedure. –
Well basically what they're doing is clocking each other's
cards. – I know. – Yes I realise that, but you know as
well as I do Geoffrey that if you pay peanuts you end up
with monkeys, it's as simple as that. – (*Laughs.*) I've got
nothing at all against monkeys. – Yes I've seen the
programmes, Geoffrey. I know they can. (*Laughs.*)

> *She notices that Tony is still in the room.*

Listen, while you're there, would you take out the three-
centimetre semi-display we have in the *Standard*. – Yes,
the post is filled. – Since today. – What? – I'm working
after work. That's what I'm doing. – Yes. Work. How's
your wife? – (*Laughs.*) Is she? – (*more laughter*) I don't
believe you, Geoffrey. – Alright. Goodbye.

> *Franky hangs up, laughs quietly, inviting Tony to
> share her amusement, but finds him preoccupied.*

What can I do for you?

Tony You're right.

Franky I'm sorry?

Tony What you said. Terry. Barbara. Then there'll be a
new person. It's not for me.

Franky OK.

,

Are you –

Tony I'm sorry. It's not fear.

,

(*with contempt*) I'm not frightened of *them*.

,

It's not the responsibility because I want the responsibility.
I can't explain.

Franky That's OK. I understand.

Tony It's not me.

,

That's all. It isn't me. Is it?

,

Well is it?

Franky I can't say. How can I say?

,

I don't think so. No.

Tony No.

Franky But listen you're welcome to think –

Tony I don't want to think. Thank you. No I don't want
to think.

Franky I understand.

Tony It's not me. This isn't me.

,

Franky I understand.

Tony You keep saying that.

,

You keep saying that.

   Blackout.

4. A Temporary Bus-Stop.

Night. Tony stands holding his present. Also waiting is a woman of similar age. They exchange a brief glance and smile. Silence. When their eyes meet again they begin to speak.

Woman Are you waiting for –

Tony A three-three-nine, that's right.

  Both faint laugh.

We may as well sleep here.

Woman I'm sorry? (*faint laugh*) Yes

Tony Joke.

Woman I know. I'm sorry.

Tony No, I'm sorry . . .

Woman No you're right.

  ,

You're absolutely right. It's only you meet . . .

Tony I frightened you.

Woman No, it's only you meet . . . Sometimes late at night . . .

Tony You can meet some pretty weird people late at night.

Woman Yes.

  Both faint laugh.

I don't know why they've had to move the stop somewhere so dark.

Tony It's only temporary.

Woman D'you think it will be permanently like this?

'

Some friends from the Institute were meant to be giving me a lift, but –

Tony But they buggered off.

Woman How did you guess.

Both faint laugh.

No really . . .

Tony Human nature . . .

Woman . . . how did you know that?

Tony What Institute is that? Is that the –

Woman I go to classes there. Crossley Road.

Tony Uh-huh.

Woman I'm involved in various things.

Tony Uh-huh. Is that right.

'

So what sort of things are various things?

Woman Well, for example, there's History.

Tony That's fascinating.

Woman This term it's the twentieth century.

'

Tony No, that's fascinating. The twentieth century. That's . . .

Woman (*dispassionate list*) Vietnam. The Holocaust.
The Atom Bomb of course. Then we go back to the
Spanish Civil War. Guernica. And of course we've done
the Somme, the Battle of the Somme . .

Tony That's a picture, isn't it.

Woman Sorry?

Tony Guernica is a picture.

Woman Is it?

,

Of course Lawrence uses a lot of visual material.
Photographs. Films.

Tony Lawrence being . . .

Woman Lawrence is our tutor.

,

Tony So, what, you memorise . . .

Woman Memorise?

Tony Memorise the dates.

Woman We try to memorise the dates. But Lawrence
doesn't really like us doing that. He's very keen on
making us think. He says he doesn't care if we've been
working all day long, we still mustn't accept what's
happened without thinking about why. Why why why.
He gets quite angry. (*faint laugh*) He's actually quite
attractive.

Tony Is he?

Woman You might've heard of him. Bott. Lawrence Bott.

Tony Lawrence Bott.

,

No. (*vague recollection*) No, actually it is familiar.

Woman He's just published a book.

,

Tony So what's he been getting angry about tonight?

Woman Tonight? No. Sorry. Tonight was French. Tuesdays is French.

Tony Right. Bonjour Mademoiselle.

Both faint laugh.

Woman What's that?

Tony It's French.

Woman I know, but what does it mean?

Tony Bonjour Mademoiselle? Well it's . . . hello. It just means hello.

Woman We haven't done that yet. What we're doing this term is we're just making the sounds. It has some beautiful sounds.

Tony The language of love.

Woman You don't go –

Tony To classes? No, but . . .

,

Woman But I suppose you have interests.

Tony Well what interests me is human nature.

Woman Human nature is fascinating.

Tony Because you can go to classes. That's one way and I respect that. But the other way is to sit tight. You observe. You compare. You don't do anything as such.

But you analyse. You analyse and over the years you find that what you accumulate . . .

Woman Is wisdom.

Tony Yes.

Both smile. Tony's increasing self-confidence has a mesmerising effect on the woman.

Hold this a minute. (*He gives her the present.*)

Woman D'you know who you're like: you're very like Lawrence.

Tony Am I? (*He presses his fingers to his temples.*)

Woman (*amused*) What're you doing?

Tony Heather.

Woman How d'you know that?

Tony Heather. Your name is Heather.

Woman How did you do that?

Tony laughs.

Woman (*laughs*) No, how did you do that?

Tony Heather. That's your name.

Woman Yes.

Tony Your name is Heather.

Woman I know. Yes. Are you psychic?

Tony What's mine?

,

Woman (*laughs*) I've no idea.

Tony You don't know my name?

Woman No. Are you famous?

Tony Anthony. Anthony Steadman. No I'm not famous.

Woman Well hello Anthony.

Tony Hello Heather.

They laugh and shake hands. Heather moves away, rubbing her bare arms. Silence. Then:

Heather Have I met you somewhere?

Tony You're cold. (*He takes off his jacket.*)

Heather No, it's nothing.

Tony No, you're cold. Your arms are cold. Come on.

Heather acquiesces and he helps her into the jacket.

It's because the sky's clear. It gets cold when the sky's clear.

Heather I must look like an idiot in this . . . Some kind of scarecrow. (*Laughing, she 'models' the jacket.*)

Tony No. Fantastic. You look fantastic.

Heather What is this anyway? (*i.e. the present which she holds*)

Tony You really do.

Heather What is this?

Tony For you. Open it.

Heather But it's yours.

Tony No. Go on. Open it.

She starts to unwrap.

It suits you.

You see there are two things. One it's my birthday. Two I've been promoted.

Heather I think someone's had this before you. It's half empty.

Tony What?

Heather I said I think someone's –

Tony Yes I heard you. What d'you mean?

Heather Look.

Tony takes the bottle, which is less than half-full.

So . . . it sounds like you've got a lot to celebrate.

Tony What's this supposed to mean?

Heather Congratulations.

Tony I mean is this supposed to be some kind of a comment?

Heather Someone's made a mistake, that's all.

Tony Terry.

Heather That's not something you could do intentionally.

Tony Because Terry can keep it.

Heather It's not important is it?

,

Tony No. I'm sorry.

Heather Terry. Is that . . . is that a girl's name?

Tony A girl? No. Terry . . . How would you describe Terry? He's just . . . one of my employees. We're obliged you see to take on a certain number of mentally handicapped people.

Heather That's very humane.

Tony Yes.

Silence. Then both faint laugh.

Look in the pockets.

Heather What?

Tony No, have a look.

She feels in the jacket pockets, while he opens the bottle.

This time I'm prepared.

Heather discovers two paper cups. She laughs.

Heather Did you *plan* this? You know, I don't normally drink spirits.

Tony (*pouring drinks*) Neither do I. I drink lager as a rule, premium lager. Cheers.

Heather Cheers. To us.

Tony To us.

Both drink. Tony immediately refills his cup.

Heather Have I met you somewhere?

Tony You've never married.

Heather Sorry?

Tony You've never –

Heather No. Married? No.

Tony I haven't.

Heather Is that a matter of principle?

Tony Absolutely not. No.

Heather You see I'm not against marriage. But interestingly enough that's an area where Lawrence and

I, we part company. Because Lawrence, he's a very right-
on sort of person, and –

Tony What's that? What's right-on?

Heather Well it means . . . I suppose it means he's
basically to the left . . .

Tony Uh-huh . . .

Heather And as someone who is basically to the left –
which I respect him for that – but he feels that a woman
shouldn't let herself be defined –

Tony This is what Lawrence feels . . .

Heather Yes. Shouldn't let herself – historically speaking –
be defined in terms of her sexual role i.e. wife, mistress,
mother. He says it's degrading. And in our class we have
these discussions where we clash. (*faint laugh*) Lawrence
and I always clash, because I say to him –

Tony Right. (*He takes the bottle.*)

Heather Look, Lawrence, a woman can't turn her back
on her sexuality any more than a man can. She can't
become neutral. Because isn't that neutrality equally
degrading? You can't ignore what you biologically are.

As Tony refills her cup.

Just a little. But Lawrence disputes that. (*faint laugh*)
I think – although of course I shouldn't say this – but
I think perhaps he has an ethnic problem.

Silence. Heather wraps the jacket around herself.

This is warm. Thank you.

,

Did you read that thing?

Tony What thing is that?

Heather It was just a thing. I read this thing where two tourists, there were two tourists, on a beach, it was on a Greek island, this is a crowded beach, and what they did was they just started to make love, I mean in front of everyone, on a crowded beach.

,

Tony That's offensive.

Heather But I don't think that it *is*, Anthony. You see I think we have to admit what we biologically are. That some things may simply be inevitable. But of course Lawrence disputes that. (*She drinks.*) And it's the same with children.

Tony I like children.

Heather So do I. I love them, because they're innocent and they're the future. But Lawrence won't hear about the future. He says: look at the world, what right do we have to a future? And each week he turns out the lights and he shows us films: cities in ruins, or human bodies being bulldozed into graves. Which is all very well. Which is all very well but we still have a right. Because each generation, each child, is another life. Is a chance to escape from that.

Tony I know exactly what you mean.

Heather Just because one generation, one life, has failed, doesn't mean that the next one will. That's not logical.

Tony No.

Heather And besides I think we all as human beings have a duty to direct people's attention away from all that ugliness.

Tony I know. There's this Complex at the back of us, it takes away all the light . . .

Heather Exactly. Architecture. (*She drinks. Confidential*) You see – personally – I don't believe that number of people died. In the gas chambers. I don't believe it's *humanly possible* for that number of people to die.

Tony I don't believe it either. I never have.

Heather It can't be.

,

Which isn't to trivialise. You see, Anthony, I think that if – like Lawrence – if you stare at ugly things for long enough, you get ugly yourself, inside. We need to show people the beautiful things. Those are the things we need to show to our children.

Tony We need to wake up.

Heather Wake up. That's beautiful. Yes.

,

Shall I tell you what I really like? I really like visiting stately homes. I've got a kind of season ticket and at the weekends I just take off. I just take off to a stately home . . .

Tony Woburn Abbey . . .

Heather The big ones naturally. But also when you apply you get a list of all the smaller ones nobody knows. So mostly it's those I visit. And that's the most beautiful thing. The most beautiful thing is to sit in one of those rooms and imagine it's mine. The plasterwork, the marble fireplaces, the gilding. Things that've lasted for hundreds of years. Mahogany floors. Do you think that's wrong?

Tony No.

Heather No it's not wrong. I know it's not wrong because I feel at home there, Anthony. What it is is a sense of confidence, of order. I can breathe. I say to myself: yes, this is me. You walk out in the gardens and what strikes you is the symmetry. Boxwood hedges. Pineapples made of stone. Round the walls there are fruit trees growing along wires. Figs. Morello cherries. Plums. In some of them they're recreating the past exactly. They're growing the same plants . . . the same species of plants. In the same places. As they were then. The same trees.

Tony That's extraordinary.

Heather So not just the house but the whole landscape is as it would've been. (*She drinks.*) I'm not making myself clear.

Tony You are. Yes you are. Landscapes. That's exactly how it should be.

Heather And it makes me think, it makes me think, Anthony, that if we could wear those clothes . . .

Tony Uh-huh . . .

Heather Or speak, speak as they did . . .

Tony Like a person of that time . . . Speak poetry . . .

Heather Because don't you ever get the feeling that the words we use . . .

Tony We can't express ourselves . . .

Heather . . . that the words we use are just the shadow of a language that we've lost. And perhaps if we could speak that language . . .

Tony I know . . .

Heather Speak poetry . . . Or dance . . .

Tony Yes . . .

Heather They could all dance . . . (*She puts down her cup and offers her hand.*) Come on.

Tony What?

Heather We can dance.

Tony Dance.

Heather Yes. Come on.

Tony You mean dance. You mean actually dance?

,

Now.

Heather I mean actually dance. Yes.

Tony (*faint laugh*) I can't.

Heather You can. (*She takes his hand.*) Of course you can. Why should we be limited by preconceived ideas about ourselves?

They begin to dance, without close physical contact, oddly graceful. Heather repeatedly hums a short slow phrase, and Tony joins in this ostinato. Time passes before Heather speaks.

In summer they have concerts. They play the music on the old instruments, the original instruments.

They continue to dance and hum.

Perhaps that's where we met.

,

Tony Where?

Heather In one of those houses, one of those rooms. In a previous life.

Both faint laugh. The dance continues until Tony breaks gently away.

Tony I need a piss.

They both laugh. While Tony finds a dark corner, Heather, still humming the tune, leans against a wall.

Heather Bonjour Mademoiselle. (*faint laugh*)

She continues to hum. Tony returns into the light. He drains the bottle into his mouth. Taking the bottle he goes to Heather and presses himself against her.

Tony Let's do it.

Heather What are you doing?

Tony Come on. Let's do it.

Heather What're you talking about?

It takes a moment for Heather to realise that Tony is in earnest. But there is no question of an ambiguous response: she is utterly terrified.

Get off me. What're you doing?

Tony Shut up. Let's just do it.

Heather Oh Jesus Christ.

Tony Come on.

Heather SOMEBODY HELP ME!

They struggle.

Tony Come on. Ease up. Relax.

He pins her against the wall.

Come on. Pull this up. Help me. Pull it up. You're not helping me.

Heather Oh Christ you're ripping . . . Help me he's insane.

Tony You see the mistake I made last time . . . I frightened you by being weak. I'm sorry.

Heather Just fuck off of me, fuck off . . .

Tony I respected you as a *person* . . .

Heather Help me . . .

Tony What I failed to see last time was that – KEEP STILL – was that I needed to assert myself . . .

Heather What d'you mean last time? What d'you mean?

Tony But this time. Look. I'm in control. Ease up, Heather. Relax. Pull this up . . .

Heather Please. It's a mistake . . .

Tony I love you. I'm in control . . .

Heather Look, you're confusing me with someone. We've never met . . .

Tony No no no. You don't understand . . .

Heather I do. I do understand, Anthony. Yes if we could just think about this, if we could just decide, just decide who it is –

Tony KEEP STILL CAN'T YOU FUCK YOU!

He smashes the bottle against the wall. Heather turns her head away in terror and closes her eyes, too afraid of the glass to fight. This sudden passivity confuses Tony.

What's wrong? Your eyes are shut. What's wrong?

'

Heather Just do it. Please, please don't hurt me. Just do it. Just do it and go away.

Tony What d'you mean?

Heather (*eyes shut*) I haven't seen you. I swear I can't describe you. Don't hurt me.

Tony What d'you mean? We've been talking. We've been dancing. What d'you mean you can't describe me?

Heather cannot speak.

Tony Open your eyes. OPEN YOUR EYES! (*He drops the piece of bottle and forces her eyes open.*) Look. It's me. Don't you remember me? This is me. Anthony. I want to marry you. We're going to have children.

Heather spits in his face.

Tony You don't mean that. I'm sorry but you don't mean that. Yes yes yes last time we missed our chance, and perhaps you feel strongly, but now it's different: I'm in control.

Heather slips away.

'

Or we could have a meal.

'

We could have a meal. We could talk.

Blackout.

Act Two

1. A Launderette.

Tony is folding shirts. Sitting apart from him is a black man wearing a shabby suit and tie, holding a briefcase. When this man begins to speak – quietly but insistently – Tony will ignore him for as long as possible. Firstly however there is silence as Tony folds.

Man Wherever we look we see a world in decay.

It may be in the silence of the forests.

It may be moral decay. It may be in our inability to say what moral means.

Or it may be disease. A shadow falling on our most intimate moments.

Whenever we turn the soil to plant or build we uncover shallow graves. At every step we stumble over bones.

We look to culture to make sense of this, only to find that what we call culture consists of faint distress signals emanating from the wreck of our beliefs.

As we feel our way forwards, we find less and less to hold on to. We are blind men climbing sheer smooth rock in the dark.

We are astonished when we calculate the enormity *of* the universe. We discover that the world consists almost entirely of time and space. Why then do we seem to have so little of either?

At every step we stumble over bones. We are surely reaching the point where it will not be possible to go on, but we choose to ignore it.

The train.

The train streaks into a mountain tunnel from which it will never emerge. Briefly there are faces at the window. The children are waving. The adults in the buffet are dithering over a selection of fresh sandwiches. White or brown. With salad or without. They are experiencing the illusion of choice.

Tony meets his glance. Silence.

I'm sorry I'm embarrassing you.

Tony faint laugh.

Man Those are mostly extracts from chapter seven. The reflections on culture are from the appendix.

Tony I see.

Man It's a theme I would've liked to develop, given the time.

Tony Uh-huh.

,

Man You have a particular way of folding your shirts.

,

One can't help noticing.

Tony I've always done it this way.

Man Do you travel much by train?

Tony Bus. Mostly by bus.

Man You've possibly heard of me.

Tony Uh-huh. I don't think so.

Man You've possibly heard of me: Bott. Lawrence Bott. (*He grasps Tony's hand.*)

Tony No. (*vague recollection*) Well no actually it does seem familiar.

Lawrence Some years ago I published a book. You might've heard of it.

Tony Uh-huh.

Lawrence *A World in Decay*. You've possibly heard of it.

Tony Sorry.

Lawrence Don't be.

,

No, don't be. I published *A World in Decay* at my own expense and distributed it with a trolley to small bookshops on a sale or return basis. Most of the copies were in fact returned. No, don't be sorry.

Tony No, I'm sorry.

Lawrence Don't be.

,

Listen. I'd like to show you something. (*He rummages in his briefcase as he speaks.*) You see a crucial experience for me was my period at the Adult Institute in Crossley Road. I was very moved by what I saw there. I was moved and angered. Across the corridor for example – in room D6 – there were grown men and women struggling to read and write. I wanted to weep for the opportunities that had been denied to them. Their ambition, their ambition was often no more than to recognise their own names. (*He gives Tony a card.*) And in my own classes – before their unfortunate closure – I taught History three times a week, which was enough to live on, in D17 – Lawrence Bott, you might've beard of me – in those classes, whose closure is still subject to appeal, in those classes, where I had expected from adults at least a sense of the cumulative horror, I found instead a calm acceptance of the past coupled with the idea that it was

a kind of never-ending classic serial, with no expense
spared on costume and the reconstruction of period
detail. There was no outrage. There was no remorse.
So what I did – and do you believe this is wrong? –
because how can it be wrong? – what I did was I began
to show them, methodically, whatever footage I could
find: of Dresden, of Hiroshima, of the crematoria of
Europe. I pointed out to them the terrible errors and
misunderstandings of History, which with hindsight
are so simply identified. I asked them to consider the
possibility – merely the possibility – that other choices
might've been made. Better choices. But no: to them the
past was like a film: frame followed frame: because it
was inevitable, it justified itself. Justified. Now that made
me really angry. I would say to them: are you seriously
trying to tell me that these things were meant to be?
That in other words they are part of a plan? Because
if you are, if you are, don't you realise you're saying
exactly the same as these fascists were, with their theories
of biological superiority, of biological destiny. Are you
seriously suggesting that these things were intended?
That they serve a purpose? How can we accept that?

'

Tony Look, it's very interesting, but really I just came in
here to dry my shirts.

Lawrence How can we accept that? Please don't trivialise.

Tony contemplates the card.

Tony So what is this?

Lawrence Yes yes yes. It may not be rational. But what
has reason achieved? Reason has constructed the train. It
has constructed the tunnel. What it has failed to provide
is an exit.

Tony Yes but what is this?

248

Lawrence This is what I'm talking about.

Tony Which is?

Lawrence Not just History. But you as a person. The opportunities you've missed. The things you regret.

Tony Which are?

Lawrence Why should frame follow frame?

Tony Which are?

Lawrence You know what they are.

,

They're there in your eyes. From your earliest memory. You know what they are. Because what do we accumulate?

Tony (*increasingly absorbed in the card*) What is this exactly?

Lawrence We accumulate wisdom only to find it's too late to apply it.

Tony Bring this number . . .

Lawrence Ring. It's a misprint. Please ring.

Tony Uh-huh. A Marabout. What is that?

Lawrence Mouhamed Lamine is a holy man and a personal friend.

Tony Uh-huh.

,

Mouhamed Lamine.

Lawrence He does not inhabit the world in a material sense.

Tony Action at a distance . . .

Lawrence Bending spoons.

Tony Spoons.

Lawrence That's just an example, a trivial example of what could be achieved.

,

Don't you see what I'm saying? If only we could go back.
   Our language tells us that this is possible: what could've been, what might've been. These are the tenses of remorse and regret, but also the tenses of endless possibility.
   If only we could go back.
   Yes. Knowing what we do now.
   Our language, if not our reason, tells us that this is possible.

,

(*passionately*) Look at us. We're not meant to be like this. We're human beings.

Tony Speak for yourself.

Lawrence We're human beings.

   Silence.

Tony Can I keep this?

Lawrence The card is yours. I make no charge for the card.

Tony Thank you.

Lawrence Thank you for listening. (*He grasps Tony's hand between his, and holds onto it.*) Do you have twenty pence?

Tony For the drier.

Lawrence For me. For a human being. Do you have twenty pence?

,

Tony But you –

Lawrence I have nothing.

Tony But you teach –

Lawrence Teach? They won't even let me past reception. They're taking evidence. They're preparing reports.

Tony No, that's terrible.

Lawrence I'm in here to keep *warm*.

Tony (*reaches into pocket*) Twenty pence. No, that's really terrible. I'm sorry.

Lawrence Don't be. Or whatever you can spare. Forty. Fifty. With fifty I can get chips. With a pound I could obtain a Special Brew, a Carlsberg Special Brew.

Tony A pound.

Lawrence Fifty pence. Whatever. Whatever you can spare. Thank you.

Tony It's nothing.

Lawrence For another pound let me present you with a signed copy of my book.

> *Lawrence gives a book to Tony, who reads from the cover.*

Tony *A World in Decay*. Thank you.

Lawrence It represents a considerable discount over the published price.

Tony pays for the book, slips Lamine's card inside, and pockets it.

I realise this is embarrassing for you, but equally it is embarrassing for me. Please don't imagine I'm acting out of choice. When you have time, read it.

Tony No. Thank you. I will.

Lawrence Bott. Lawrence Bott. You might've heard of me.

Tony I have to go.

Lawrence I'm in here to keep warm.

Tony I'm sorry but I have to go now.

Lawrence I accept that.

>

Tony I have to take back these shirts and put them in a drawer.

Lawrence Of course. I accept that.

>

Blackout.

2. The Pub.

Nick plays the fruit machine. Tony sits in the shadows staring at or through Kate, who is also lost in thought. Eventually he comes over to her, indifferent to the fact that she ignores him.

Tony No, I see what this must look like, but it isn't what you think. I mean I'm not making a play for you or anything. I'm aware that you have commitments and

I respect that. If I'm drawn to you – and I am – it's because I'm drawn to you as a couple. You make a very attractive couple. (*as if she were about to speak*) No, please, I think these things should be said.

I've always thought: I know her from somewhere, we've met. We've spoken before. But now I see that what it is is you're very like somebody. You've heard that before. Of course. But you genuinely are. You're genuinely like Franky where I work. Which is short for Frances. By which I don't mean to belittle you. Because of course you're unique. We're all of us unique. I'm just talking about a resemblance.

,

Perhaps I'm intruding – and if I am forgive me – but I've been doing a lot of thinking this evening. I've been sitting over there. You've probably noticed me. It's where I normally sit. I've been thinking about the past, and watching you both, and I find myself drawn.

,

I've been trying to think of my earliest memory. What's your earliest memory? I think mine is wearing red plastic sandals. It's summer and I'm wearing red plastic sandals. I'm looking at the sky and I notice that it's full of little bright specks, like sparks.

,

I asked my teacher: what are the little bright specks I can see? She told me: those are germs.

,

Do you think she really believed they were germs?

Faint smile from Kate, who looks at him for the first time.

And if not, what was she trying to do to me? I'd like to ask her that.

,

You see I've been watching you both. Not in that sense. No if I wanted to watch that – which I don't – I could go and pay for it. But I've been watching you both, and what I observe is that you don't talk to each other.

Which perhaps means that you don't need to – which is all very well – it's all very well, but it makes me curious. And stop me, please stop me if you feel I'm intruding but it makes me curious as to what you really feel.

,

You don't talk. Now maybe that's love. I'd like to think so. But maybe there's something else. Something that eats away at you inside. That's all. I only ask because I'm curious as to what you really feel. Perhaps it eats away at you. And maybe if you talked . . .

,

Because you're welcome to come back. Both of you are welcome to come back with me and talk. It's a small place, but if you don't mind sitting on the bed . . .

Nick has joined them.

Nick Excuse me.

Tony This isn't what you think.

Nick Excuse me.

,

Tony No, I just want to talk. I'm not . . . listen, I'm not *suggesting* anything.

Nick You want to talk.

Tony To both of you.

Nick We're not interested.

Tony This isn't what you think.

Nick How d'you know what I think?

Tony I mean if it was sexual . . .

Nick How d'you know what I think?

Tony I'm not saying I *know*.

Nick Then what are you saying?

Tony That's not what I'm saying.

,

Nick Has he been saying anything to you?

Kate shrugs.

Tony For example: perhaps you want children, but are unable to.

Nick You're joking.

Tony Maybe that's why you don't talk to each other . . .

Nick Listen . . .

Tony . . . i.e. there's a void . . .

Nick Listen . . .

Tony . . . or maybe you look at the world and say: what right do we have? I can understand that.

Nick Crap.

Tony Because we're blind. We're climbing rocks in the dark.

Nick Crap.

Tony I respect that. Alright. I respect that.

Nick There's nothing wrong with the *world*.

Tony OK.

  '

OK. I respect that. It's debatable. But if that's so – maybe it's so – but let me ask you a question.

Nick You want to ask me a question.

Tony Yes. What is there that you regret?

Nick What?

Tony What do you regret?

  '

Nick Nothing.

Tony What d'you mean nothing?

Nick I mean nothing.

  Kate and Nick exchange a faint laugh.

Tony No, listen: I'm talking about the things you've done in your life.

Nick Right. So what's wrong with your life?

Tony No, I'm not asking you . . .

Nick I know that.

Tony . . . to tell me, to tell me what's wrong with my life.

Nick I know that.

  '

So let's leave it.

Tony What I'm asking you is if you've ever regretted anything. Yourself as a person.

Nick As a person.

Tony Because I'm not asking you to tell me what's wrong with my life. Because alright I know what's wrong with it. I have insight into that.

Nick Uh-huh.

,

You're taking it too seriously.

Tony What?

Nick You're taking it –

Tony My life. I'm taking it too seriously.

Nick You've put your finger on it.

Tony Well thank you very much.

,

Nick There you are.

Tony Thank you very much.

Nick There you are. Look at yourself. You're taking it too seriously.

Tony Well thank you. Fuck you as a matter of fact.

Nick That's fine.

Tony Fuck you.

,

Nick My pleasure.

Tony Because whoever you are . . .

Kate All the world's a stage.

Tony . . . you're not in a position to pass judgement.

Nick Really.

Kate We're actors. The world's a stage.

Tony I'm sorry, but that's a meaningless remark.

Nick She's right.

Kate We strut. We fret.

Nick She's right.

Tony No, I'm sorry but she isn't right. How can that be right? I mean this isn't an act. This is me. I'm here. I'm making decisions. I could've stayed over there where I normally sit but no I've come over here of my own free will to speak to you both because I have something to say. An actor is repeating a part, but this is different, this is entirely different.

,

This is significant. This is me.

Kate It's a tale told by an idiot.

Tony Is that supposed to be a comment?

Kate Signifying nothing.

Tony Is that supposed to be some kind of a comment?

,

Well is it?

Nick Leave it.

Kate It's actually poetry.

Nick Let's leave it.

Tony Poetry.

Nick This is an actress. You're talking to an actress.

,

Tony What's that – a professional actress?

Kate I'm Kate. Yes.

Tony I'm sorry. Hello Kate.

Kate Hello.

Tony Anthony. And I apologise. Because I respect your profession.

Kate Thank you.

Tony But as an actress – whatever kind of actress you are – I know that you'll have insight into human nature.

Nick I'll tell you what I do regret.

,

Tony Because that's your job.

Nick I'll tell you what I do regret.

Tony I'd like you to.

Nick What I regret, my friend, is the fact that you exist.

Kate laughs and puts her arm around Nick.

Kate He doesn't mean that.

Tony No that's absolutely fine by me. Because I take that –

Nick Don't I?

Tony I take that in the spirit in which it was intended.

Nick No offence.

Tony That is to say i.e. as an example. A trivial example. Absolutely. None taken.

Nick and Kate kiss. Tony continues as if he had their attention.

Because no one's denying, Kate, that we learn from our mistakes. And I accept your point that a poet can turn that into poetry. That's fine. But for the rest of us who are not poets which is the vast majority, by the time we've learned from our mistakes it's already too late. Those opportunities will never return. And even if you study life, even if you write books about it, you can still find yourself in the launderette, not to do your washing, I mean just to keep *warm*.

Kate slips away.

Where's she going?

Nick What d'you mean?

Tony Katy. Where's Katy going?

Nick She's going to the toilet.

Tony OK. Fine.

Nick She's just going to the toilet.

Tony No, that's fine.

   ,

Listen –

Nick You have something against that?

Tony No. Listen. How old am I?

Nick (*shrugs*) Forty?

Tony How did you know that?

   ,

That's exactly right. I'm thirty-nine, and tomorrow I'll be forty.

Nick Crisis in other words.

Tony No, are you psychic?

Nick Congratulations.

Tony What? No. Not congratulations.

Nick OK.

Tony Not congratulations, because . . .

,

Because. Alright?

Nick Because.

Tony Because I will be forty years old tomorrow, and over those forty years, what have I accumulated?

Nick (*shrugs*) Money?

Tony Money, no.

,

No I'm not speaking in a material sense.

Nick Give up.

Tony Wisdom.

Nick Wisdom.

Tony Yes, we accumulate wisdom, but what use is it to us? Because the events when the wisdom would've been useful, they're over and gone.

Nick Well then that's how it is.

Tony No that's *not* how it is.

Nick Well then I'm sorry, I don't understand what you're saying.

Tony That's alright.

,

No that's alright. I accept that because what I'm trying to say is not rational.

Nick It's not rational.

Tony No.

,

Nick Fine.

Tony I mean how old are you?

,

Nick Why? Twenty-eight.

Tony And what's your profession?

Nick My profession?

Tony Yes, what do you do?

Nick Do I have a job?

Tony Yes.

Nick (*faint laugh*) No.

Tony In other words you missed the opportunity. The opportunity was there, but at the crucial moment you said to yourself: this isn't me.

Nick What opportunity?

Tony To work. To get a job. Because if that opportunity presented itself again – and what I'm suggesting to you is that that could be possible – you wouldn't say: this isn't me. You'd seize it. You wouldn't be coming here . . .

Nick I happen to like coming here . . .

Tony Night after night.

Nick I like coming here.

Tony You like coming here.

,

Don't deceive yourself.

Kate returns.

Don't deceive yourself. You and Katy here make an attractive couple, as I was saying. But why does an attractive couple come in here night after night to drink this stuff and sit in basically silence?

,

Nick It's Anthony's birthday.

Kate Congratulations Anthony.

Tony Tomorrow. Thank you.

Kate Are you doing anything?

Tony Tomorrow? Not doing as such. No.

As Tony drains his glass, Kate whispers to Nick.

Nick (*prompted by Kate*) Look, d'you want another drink, Tone?

Tony Sorry?

Nick Your birthday. You want a –?

Kate Well of course he does.

Tony A drink? Well yes, if you're . . .

Nick Pils?

Tony Holsten Pils. Thank you very much.

Nick This dead?

Tony Thanks. Thanks a lot.

Nick goes with the empties. Silence punctuated by faint fruit machine.

Fantastic. You look fantastic.

Kate faint laugh.

Tony You have a lovely face.

Kate Thank you.

Tony Have I said that before?

Kate No.

Tony Because I know I have a habit, I know I've a habit of repeating myself.

Kate You didn't say that before.

Tony Good, that's good. You have a lovely face.

Kate Thank you.

Tony You have a lovely face, but you've still failed. Why is that?

Kate (*faint laugh*) I haven't failed.

Tony Of course you've failed. Look.

Kate What?

Tony It's there in your eyes.

'

Kate Listen, I –

Tony I didn't want to say that but it's there in your eyes, Kate. What does an actress do in the evenings? An actress works. She's known. I mean Kate what? Kate who? If you weren't here what difference would it make to anything? And naturally you persuade yourself that there is an intention, that it's meant to be like this, it's meant to be. But what does meant to be mean? Meant to be doing the same thing for eighteen years? Meant to be keeping warm next to a clothes-drier while someone writes reports? No way.

,

No way, Kate. Meant to be means nothing.

Kate What reports?

Tony Because listen, what are we, you and I?

Kate Wait a minute, wait a minute. Don't include me in this.

Tony We're human beings.

Kate Don't include me.

Tony We're human beings. And perhaps I'm repeating myself, but for human beings everything should be possible. The language we speak tells us that. It tells us that the potential – by which I mean not only what we could be, but what we might've been – the potential is infinite. And so what's *meant* to happen – which is surely the realisation of that potential – are you with me? – what's meant to happen, hasn't happened. And what *has* happened – what's happened to us – was not meant to happen. No.

,

How can we believe that about ourselves? Because listen –

Kate I'm listening

Tony OK.

,

Yes?

Kate I'm listening to you.

Tony Good.

Kate No, I'm interested.

Tony Well you should be.

Kate I am. What are you suggesting?

Tony That's good. Because listen, I normally sit over there and every night I see you, the two of you, over here, and don't you understand my heart bleeds.

Kate And if I happen to like it here?

Tony It bleeds for you. What d'you mean: like it here? That's exactly what *he* said. (*Picks up a bottle.*) Don't you know what this stuff is doing to your body? If you got pregnant? What sort of baby you might have?

Kate (*betraying sadness*) That's unlikely.

Tony Exactly.

,

Yes, exactly.

Kate So what are you suggesting?

Tony (*intensely*) What I'm suggesting, Kate, is that there is a train. It's going into the tunnel. The children are waving.

,

I'm suggesting that if we could only go *back*.

,

   Kate faint laugh.

Tony Yes.

Kate You can't go back.

Tony Yes, but if only we could. Live our lives again.
Knowing what we do now. Knowing that. Don't you see?

*As Nick approaches with new bottles, Tony takes a
piece of paper from his pocket and passes it to Kate.*

Kate What's this?

Tony No, look at it.

*While Nick gives Tony a bottle, Kate unfolds the
paper.*

Cheers.
That's right. Look at it.

Nick What is it?

Kate (*reads*) 'Custom Coils Farringdon Road. Friendly
family firm requires . . .'

Tony No no no . . .

Kate '. . . requires supervisor for specialist workshop.'
So?

Tony Not that. I don't mean that.

Tony feels in his pockets. He gets out the book.

Kate (*to Nick*) Have you seen the date on this? Look:
it's falling apart.

Tony I don't mean that. I had a card. He gave me a
card.

Kate 'Telephone Frances Wood.'

Nick has hold of the book.

Tony Mouhamed Lamine. It was in there.

Nick (*reads*) 'Wherever we look we see a world in
decay.'

267

Kate (*laughs*) What?

Nick 'It may be in the silence of the forests. It may be moral decay.'

Tony It was in there.

Nick 'It may be in our inability to say what moral means.' (*He laughs and tosses down the book.*)

Tony No. Lamine. Mouhamed Lamine.

Kate Gave you the book?

Tony No. A card. He gave me a card. Lawrence gave me a card. It was in there.

Nick How can you read that stuff?

Tony It was in there.

Nick Well don't look at me.

'

Don't look at me.

Tony Will you please return it.

Nick What?

Tony Yes. I'm asking you to return my card.

Nick (*walking away*) What card? I'm sorry but I don't believe this. This is not in fact happening.

Tony You're not walking away. You're not walking away with something that is mine by rights.

Nick Will someone please tell this person –

Tony DON'T WALK AWAY FROM ME!

> *Tony seizes Nick. A brief but very violent struggle. Nick produces a knife and stabs Tony dead. After a short silence Kate realises that the knife has fallen.*

Kate (*softly*) Pick it up.

Nick (*faint laugh of disbelief*) Something so trivial . . .

Kate Pick it up.

'

Nick (*with difficulty*) I don't regret this.
Why do people have to talk?

With great reluctance, Kate recovers the knife.

What makes them start conversations? What do they expect to achieve? What's wrong?

Kate Just take it. (*She gives him the knife.*)

Nick I like coming here. I like *being* here.

'

I don't regret this. There's nothing wrong with the *world*. The man is dreaming.

Kate tries to move Nick away.

Kate Come on.

Nick Don't patronise me. Don't patronise me. I'm in control.

Kate Yes yes yes. Alright. Come on.

Nick I am. I'm in control. (*faint laugh*)

Kate I know. Come on. Move.

'

Move now.

Neither moves.
Blackout.

3. Custom Coils: The·Workshop.

Supervisor Marc is inspecting stock, making notes on a clipboard, taking his time. His back is turned to Barbara, who stacks boxes of components. Both wear surgical hats. The phone is ringing. For a while no one speaks.

Barbara Marc.

    ,

Marc, it's the phone.

   Phone continues to ring.

Marc Will you answer the phone.

Barbara (*quietly rising hysteria*) Marc. I'm busy. I'm trying to do this.

    ,

I can't be in two places at once, Marc. The phone isn't my responsibility. I'm trying to do this. I haven't slept all night. I'm upset. I've had nightmares. I called the doctor but it was just a recorded message. Then you ask me to answer the phone. I mean are you trying to make me overdose again, Marc? Is that what you're trying to do?

   Phone continues to ring. Marc's back remains turned.

Do you want to have that on your conscience? Because I feel very close to it this morning. I feel very close to it, Marc. And all it needs is for people to start making demands –

   Barbara drops a box. She exclaims and immediately begins to cry. The components scatter. Marc takes no obvious notice of this. After a moment he goes and answers the phone.

Marc Custom Coils . . .

*But the caller has hung up. Marc replaces the receiver.
He contemplates Barbara, then goes up to her.*

(*gently*) Barbara . . . Barbara . . .

*He takes out a handkerchief. Barbara takes it and
wipes her eyes. She looks up. They both smile. She
clutches his arm. They separate and return to their
tasks, Barbara putting the components back in the
box.*
    Terry enters, in surgical hat.

Terry Morning.

*No reaction from Marc or Barbara. Terry takes a
piece of paper out of his pocket.*

(*tentatively*) Marc . . . when you have time, mate . . .
perhaps we could . . . go over this together. OK?

,

So what is this then? A minute's silence or what?

*Franky enters. She lights a cigarette. Terry helps
Barbara clear up. This proceeds in silence. Franky
makes one or two aimless moves: there's no reason for
her to be in the room. After a while she takes a
magazine from under a pair of ear-cans.*

Franky *Country Life?* (*faint laugh*) Whose is this?

Barbara It's Tony's.

,

Franky Tony's. Uh-huh. Right.

,

Terry Yes he was cutting out pictures, wasn't he.

Franky Was he.

Barbara He was cutting out pictures of houses. Stately homes.

Barbara, Terry and Marc all exchange a glance at this. A faint laugh ripples round.

Franky No music.

,

Terry So what, you going to . . . you going to advertise?

Barbara For godsake Terry . . .

,

Franky Advertise, no, I think we're managing. That's right, isn't it Marc: we're managing?

Marc That's right. We're managing.

Franky Good.

,

Managing, no, that's very good. Let's have some music, Terry.

Terry moves to the radio.

Barbara I've just been telling Marc, Miss Wood, I still can't sleep. I have nightmares, recurring nightmares, and when you ring the doctor all you get is an answering machine. I'm wondering how long I can go on, how long I can –

The radio cuts her off: a loud driving rhythm that prevents conversation. Franky smokes, remains in the room. The others resume their tasks. They surrender to the relentless optimism of the music.

THE TREATMENT

*Life as we know it has ended, and yet no one
is able to grasp what has taken its place . . . Slowly
and steadily, the city seems to be consuming itself.*

Paul Auster
In the Country of Last Things

*The genuine pain that keeps everything awake
is a tiny, infinite burn
on the innocent eyes of other systems.*

Life is no dream. Watch out! Watch out! Watch out!

Lorca
Poet in New York

*'It's really wonderful,' said Karl.
'Developments in this country are always rapid,'
said his uncle, breaking off the conversation.*

Kafka
America

The Treatment was first performed at the Royal Court Theatre, London, on 15 April 1993, with the following cast:

Jennifer Sheila Gish
Anne Jacqueline Defferary
Andrew Larry Pine
Nicky Geraldine Somerville
Clifford Tom Watson
Simon Mark Strong
Taxi Driver Marcus Heath
John Joseph Mydell

All other parts played by members of the company

Director Lindsay Posner
Designer Julian McGowan
Lighting Designer Thomas Webster
Composer Paddy Cunneen
Sound Steve Hepworth

Characters

Jennifer, forties
Andrew, forties
Anne, twenties
Simon, twenties
Clifford, sixties
Nicky, twenties
John, forties
Taxi Driver, sixties

also

Waitress
Police Officer
Female Movie Star
Maid
Mad Woman

John, the Police Officer and the Taxi Driver
are black (African) Americans

The play is organised so that the secondary parts can if
necessary be taken by the actors playing Nicky and John

A crowd is required in Act Four, Scene One.
If a real crowd is not feasible, it must be presented
or implied by non-naturalistic means

Time and Place

The place is New York City, the time the present

ACT ONE
A day in June ·

ACT TWO
Evening of the same day

ACT THREE
A few days later

ACT FOUR
A year later

Notes

An oblique stroke / indicates the point of interruption
in overlapping dialogue

Brackets ( ) indicate momentary changes of tone
(usually a drop in projection)

A pause is denoted throughout by a comma
on a separate line

Act One

1. TriBeCa. The Office.

Anne, Jennifer and Andrew. Andrew smokes.

Jennifer So he comes right over to you.

Anne He comes right over to me.

Jennifer He comes over to you. *I* see.

Anne And he sticks tape over my mouth.

Jennifer OK. Why?

Anne To silence me. He wants to silence me.

Jennifer To silence you.

Anne Yes.

Jennifer Good. What kind of tape?

Anne Sticky tape. The kind of sticky tape you use for securing cables.

Jennifer Good.

Anne D'you know the kind / I mean?

Jennifer We know the kind / you mean.

Anne The kind with a silver back. Sometimes silver, sometimes it's black.

Jennifer Silver is good. The glint of it. That's good.

Anne He always has this tape on account of his job.

Jennifer Which is? (*to Andrew*) The way the silver would catch the light.

Anne OK. Yes. He's an electrical engineer.

Jennifer *That's* cool.

Anne So he always has this tape.

Jennifer *That's* cool. Do you struggle?

Anne *Inwardly* I struggle.

Jennifer Good.

Anne *Inwardly* I struggle. But he has a knife and calls me a bitch.

Jennifer He calls you a bitch.

Anne Yes.

Jennifer And there he is, with the knife, with the tape, this kind of tape with the silver back that's used for securing cables.

Anne Exactly.

,

Yes. / Exactly.

Jennifer So what does he do? He cuts off a length of the tape?

Anne Cuts? No.

Jennifer Uh-huh?

Anne That kind of tape / you can tear it

Jennifer *I* understand.

Anne with your fingers. In fact I would say it is *designed* to be torn.

Jennifer I understand. So he tears off a length (which is after all less awkward) / and sticks it

Anne Exactly.

Jennifer over your mouth.

Anne Yes.

Jennifer To silence you.

Anne Yes.

Jennifer This is in your home.

Anne Yes.

Jennifer On Avenue X.

Anne Yes.

Jennifer glances at Andrew.

Jennifer And the knife?

Anne And the knife?

Jennifer What does he do with the knife?

Anne The knife isn't visible.

Jennifer Uh-huh. Not visible. OK.

Anne It's more the sense, the *sense* / of a knife.

Jennifer The sense of a knife.

Anne Yes.

Jennifer But this knife, the knife that is sensed (she senses a knife), is this a part of his array?

Anne His array? What is that?

Jennifer The array of items – tools – required by his job.

Anne You mean like the tape.

Jennifer Exactly.

Anne I'm not sure.

Jennifer OK.

Anne Because as I say I only sense it. And whether or not it's part of his array is beside the point because it's then that he begins to speak.

Jennifer He speaks. He speaks to you.

Anne He speaks to me.

Jennifer OK. (The knife worries me / a little.)

Anne He speaks to me. Yes.

Jennifer How?

Anne How does he speak?

Jennifer Tell me (yes) how he speaks.

Anne OK. Well, he's rapt.

Jennifer Good. I see. No. Explain. What, this is rapt as in . . .?

Anne Rapt as in rapture.

Jennifer OK. Rapture.

Anne Rapt as in (I don't know . . .)

Jennifer Rapture is fine.

Anne Or ecstasy I suppose.

Jennifer We're happy with rapture. Unless you mean – d'you mean? – is what you mean that he is in some kind of trance. (The thought just / occurs to me.)

Anne A trance. Yes.

Jennifer That's cool. He's speaking to her as if in a trance.

Anne More *from* a trance. As if *from* a trance. As if he's just . . .

Jennifer Waking?

Anne Waking, yes, from / a trance.

Jennifer The silver tape. The glint from the light. The mirror image perhaps of his face – distorted – in the strip of tape. Tell me, has he been drinking?

Anne He doesn't drink.

Jennifer Really?

Anne Not at these moments. *Later* he drinks. Later he goes out and drinks with his friends – Holly, Joel . . .

Jennifer But now he begins to speak.

Anne Yes.

Jennifer And what does he begin to speak about?

Anne He begins to speak about a parking-lot.

Jennifer A parking-lot. OK. Does he? Which parking-lot is that?

Anne I don't know. It's outside a big store. At night. He talks about it at night. The white lines.

Jennifer The white lines.

Anne The white lines that separate the cars.

Jennifer OK.

Anne How they look at night when the cars aren't there.

Jennifer Under the lights.

Anne Exactly. Those kind of orange lights they have at night.

Jennifer Which now – OK, *I* see – *reveal* the previously concealed pattern of lines.

Anne Yes. And the low beds that divide the rows.

Jennifer These are, what, these are beds of flowers?

Anne Flowerbeds. Yes. Which also have young trees in them. He describes how they look at night.

Jennifer How the young trees look at night under the orange lights.

Anne Exactly.

Jennifer Good.

Anne The appearance of the leaves.

,

Jennifer And this is why he's silenced you.

Anne And there's a dog.

Jennifer In the room?

Anne In the distance. It sounds distressed as if the dog's / locked in.

Jennifer So let me see if I've got this right. He's silenced you and now – what? he's telling? is he telling? he's telling if I've got this right he's telling the story of the women that he – here in this parking-lot – he has – what? – abused?

Anne I'm sorry.

Jennifer Abused? Women I mean? Beneath the lights et cetera et cetera – the young trees et cetera et cetera – the white lines.

Anne No. I'm sorry. He's abused no one.

Jennifer Uh-huh? No one? Only called you a bitch. Only sealed your mouth. Only threatened you with this knife which you as you say you sense.

Anne He's abused no one. This isn't what he talks about.

Jennifer OK. But you are – would it be fair to say you are nevertheless terrified. Your eyes. (*to Andrew*) Somehow I imagine her eyes closed in terror.

Anne My eyes are *open* in terror.

Jennifer Open in terror is good. Her eyes – yes – are open, wide open staring.

Anne Absolute terror. Yes.

Jennifer They're staring – of *course* they are – they're staring into his face.

Anne His hood.

Jennifer What?

Anne Not face. He has a hood.

Jennifer OK.

Anne A kind of leather hood.

Jennifer OK. A leather hood. OK. Does he?

Jennifer and Andrew exchange a look.

I see.

Anne And he continues to talk about the beauty of the world. *That's* his theme.

Jennifer The world. Which world is that? What theme?

Anne This world.

Jennifer You mean the world, this world we are / living in?

Anne This world we are / living in.

Jennifer You don't mean some specific sub-world such as the insect world or let's say art – 'the world of Vermeer'.

Anne No. This world. The world we inhabit. Its beauty. That's his theme.

,

Jennifer OK so this man is weird.

Anne No, he's quite ordinary. I don't think of him / as weird.

Jennifer Ordinary is better. It's better (you're right) than weird. He is weird – obviously – but he *seems* ordinary. (*to Andrew*) That can work.

Anne No he seems ordinary because he is ordinary. He is profoundly ordinary.

Jennifer I might dispute that.

Anne That's what terrifies me.

Jennifer His ordinariness. I see. I *think* I see. *Perhaps* I see. But what do *you* say?

Anne Say?

Jennifer Yes. He talks a lot. This 'ordinary' guy. But what do *you* say? What's your *response*?

Anne I have tape over my mouth.

Jennifer Of course. Sorry.

Anne I can't speak.

Jennifer I'm sorry.

Anne How can I speak with tape over my mouth? Aren't you listening to me?

Jennifer Naturally you can't talk. Of *course* we're listening. So then – what? – he . . . strips you, touches you?

Anne I'm sorry.

Jennifer The man, this man, he touches you?

Anne No.

Jennifer *Inwardly* you struggle, but he overwhelms you, strips you, touches you.

Anne He just talks.

Jennifer But as he talks he's touching your body, because the beauty of your body is part of the *world's* beauty. (*to Andrew*) We see her *body,* we see the / hood.

Anne He doesn't touch my body.

Jennifer OK. Fine. (I see . . .) But he is . . . (I think I see now) he is forcing *you* to touch *him.*

Anne Not at all. No. There's no physical / contact.

Jennifer He wants *his* body to be touched, admired.

Anne There's no physical contact.

Jennifer But how can that be?

Anne It's just how it is.

Jennifer No physical contact.

Anne Zero.

,

Jennifer OK.

Anne Then he goes out.

Jennifer With Holly, with Joel.

Anne With his friends. Yes.

Jennifer Are you *sure* about that?

   Anne looks away. Silence. Jennifer glances at Andrew.

OK why don't we break for lunch here. Andrew?

Andrew Japanese?

Jennifer D'you like Japanese, Anne? Sushi?

Anne Sushi . . . that's . . .

Andrew It's fish, raw fish. Have you never had sushi?

Jennifer There's a place not far from here. Why don't we walk, get some / air.

Andrew Sushi is an art.

Jennifer It's unpretentious. You'll like it.

Andrew We like it.

Jennifer You'll like it. It's quiet. I should think you like quiet places, don't you Anne.

Anne I like clearings, clearings in a forest. Yes. I do. How did you know that?

Andrew It's not as quiet as a clearing.

Anne I understand that.

Andrew It's a restaurant.

Anne Of course.

Jennifer (*into intercom*) Nicky, have I had any messages?

Nicky's Voice You're meeting Webb at two.

Jennifer (*intercom*) Who the hell is Webb? We shan't be here / at two.

Andrew There's a certain amount of noise in a restaurant – there has to be.

Anne Orders. Conversation.

Andrew Exactly.

Jennifer (*intercom*) We're taking Anne to lunch right now. He'll just have / to wait.

Andrew What there is is a background, a constant background.

Anne It's like that in the forest too.

Jennifer OK, let's go.

Andrew Shall we go? (*He follows Anne out, talking to her.*) In the forest. Really? Is it?

2. Canal Street and Broadway. The Sidewalk.

An elderly man, Clifford, is selling dishes and other household goods arranged on a blanket. A young man, Simon, picks through the items. He's drinking from a bottle of beer inside a brown paper bag.

Clifford I mapped out the course of my life very early on – in the fifties in fact. In the fifties I must've been your age, but already / I had decided

Simon How much is this?

Clifford (*that one's ten*) I had decided that I would divide each year of my life into two halves. In one half of the year I would do whatever was necessary to live – usually as it turned out in the summer months – meatpacking on Tenth and Fourteenth (of course I was stronger then) – or maybe / waiting tables

Simon And this?

Clifford (*fifteen*) last year for example I was security
guard at the Museum of Modern Art because in recent
years I've generally looked for something air-conditioned.
And these modest jobs have given / me the means

Simon Fifteen for a *plate*?

Clifford to live because my outgoings are very low. That
is Limoges. It belonged to my parents. It is not 'a plate',
it is Limoges. And then the rest of the year, *each* year
(the forks and spoons are solid silver) each and every
year what I've done – generally through the winter
months, the fall and winter months – is I've risen early,
often in the dark, and I've sat at my desk, which
is mahogany and belonged to my father and which I
would never sell even though it fills my room and I have
to sleep curled up under it – I've sat at my father's desk –
he lost everything in '29 the year I was born – I've sat at
that desk and every year without fail I have completed
a play. That's forty-one shows in as many years. Now
there's a word for that. The word my young friend is
discipline.

Simon Discipline. Uh-huh. Is it?

Clifford As a young man I had a couple of big hits in
the fifties.

> *Simon smiles. He's not listening. He examines the
> silver.*

You don't believe me? In the fifties a couple of my shows
were playing on Broadway. I have the programmes right
here. (*He pulls out some tattered programmes.*) You
see – big stars – *my* name. And when I say Broadway I
mean uptown – proper theatres – not these holes that call
themselves theatres where people who call themselves

actors mouth the obscenities of people who call themselves writers. (*He chuckles*.) Two shows on Broadway. Then after that, nothing.

He folds up the programmes and puts them away.

Simon I like this fork.

Clifford Does that seem just to you? Is that justice?

Simon How much for the fork?

Clifford To dedicate your life to something, to an *art*.

Simon How much is the fork?

,

Clifford I'll take five for the fork. I send out scripts. Once in a while I have a meeting with a young person like yourself who tells me my work is old-fashioned. I say to them that's also true of William Shakespeare. (*He chuckles*.)

Simon Uh-huh? You say five?

Clifford It's antique.

Simon I'll take it. (*He pays*.)

Clifford I can see you value things like this, beautiful things like this.

Clifford pockets the five. He looks at Simon.

It's unusual to find someone on the street who values these things.

,

Perhaps you know someone who . . .
   I mean could introduce me to someone who . . .
   Because I have *meetings* / but I never –

Simon I have no interest in the theatre.

,

Clifford I see.

Simon I have no interest in any form of art.

Clifford Which is your right. I see that.

Simon I will not pay good money to be told that the world is a heap of shit.

Clifford Listen, I write comedies. I've no / intention of –

Simon I won't sit in the dark to be told that it is an unweeded garden.

Clifford A garden.

Simon An unweeded (that's right) garden. Or that man is man's – OK? – excrement. And these are men who have supposedly *thought* would you believe about the world, men who are respected, who have a place in *history* . . .

Clifford Our own excrement? Is that *Biblical*?

Simon But what I say to them *is*, is the world is not a heap of shit, *you* my friend are the heap of shit . . .

   Nearby a car alarm goes off.

. . . the world is not a heap of shit because the sickness is *in here* . . .

Clifford In the brain. OK. Listen –

Simon Right here – yes – in the brains of those individuals. People who practise so-called *art,* who urinate on their responsibility to others in order to burrow down into themselves, to drag up stories *out* of themselves.

Clifford You mean it's a chemical? Have you *studied* this?

Simon It could be a chemical, it could be an *experience* they've had.

The alarm grows more piercing.

Clifford In the womb.

Simon Wherever.

Clifford (Because I believe that people *do have* experiences / in the womb.)

Simon Wherever. It could be chemical. It could be their environment. But all I would say to them is get off of my back. Get the fuck off of my back because I do not *need* that.

The alarm is piercing. Anne, Jennifer and Andrew are passing on their way to the restaurant. Simon catches sight of Anne.

Anne?
Anne! Stop!

Anne and her companions stop. She stares at Simon.

It's me. Simon.

Jennifer Who *is* that?

Anne I've no idea.

No one speaks. The alarm sounds.

Simon (*to Anne*) Who are those people?

Anne I don't know you. I'm sorry.

Simon But it's Anne? You *are* Anne?

Anne I think you're mistaken.

Andrew Come along, Anne. We should go.

He tries to move her on.

Jennifer This neighbourhood's not safe. We should've gotten a cab. (*to Anne*) I'm so *sorry*.

Andrew We should go, Anne.

They move on, but Anne continues to stare back at Simon.

Simon ANNE!

Andrew Just keep moving. Are you OK?

Simon ANNE!

They've gone. The alarm still sounds.

That was Anne. That was my wife. I'm sure that was my wife. Only she's changed something – her hair – her clothes. What has she *done* to herself? Who were those *people*?

Car alarm stops.

They called her Anne. Didn't you hear them call her Anne?

Clifford Who is Anne?

Simon Anne is my wife.

A police officer appears. Simon is too absorbed to notice, but Clifford immediately begins bundling his things up in the blanket.

Simon She is my wife. Where are they taking her?

Officer There's a child in the trunk of that blue Plymouth. Chinese, male, about eight years old. He's been shot through the back of the head. He has no face.

Has either of you seen a Chinese male about eight
years old?
Did either of you hear a shot?
Did either of you hear a car security alarm?

Silence.
The officer notices that the paper bag has fallen
from the bottle which Simon still holds. He picks up
the bag and thrusts it in Simon's face.

What's this?

Simon It's a bag.

Officer And what is this?

Simon It's a bottle, a bottle of beer.

Officer SO PUT THE FUCKING BOTTLE IN THE
BAG YOU FUCKHEAD.
YES YOU YOU ASSHOLE.
I'M TALKING TO YOU.
THE BOTTLE.
IN THE BAG.

3. A Japanese Restaurant.

Anne sits with Andrew at a table for three.

Andrew I'll tell you what excites us, Anne. It's because
you're of the here and now. You're in the moment and *of*
the moment. You're *real*. Because what are people *doing*
out there? Out there they are listening to Schubert on
authentic pianos. They are singing Bach at A-four-fifteen.
They are squeezing into costumes, Anne, and mouthing
words from old books. They are journeying on highly-
polished steam-trains, looking tearfully out of the

windows at a landscape to which one day they will no doubt return – older, wiser, immaculately lit. (*He smiles at Anne, pours her a drink.*) These are people, Anne, who are allergic to the time we are living in. They can't eat the food. They can't touch another's body. They can't breathe the air. Their lives must be spent behind a screen or they will have a respiratory *crisis.*

Anne sips the wine.

These are people who've given up. They say, 'We do not have words to describe this state of affairs, this state of the world.' They say, 'Words fail us.' But words can't fail, Anne, only *we* can fail.

Anne sips the wine. A waitress enters with dishes. Andrew lowers his voice.

I love you, Anne.

Waitress K?

Andrew K is mine.

Waitress G?

Andrew G is for Jennifer. She's sitting here. (*The empty seat.*)

Waitress F?

Anne doesn't react.

F? (*Waitress puts dish F in front of Anne and goes.*)

Anne I'm sorry? You *love* me?

Andrew Yes, Anne. Yes, I do.

She laughs softly in embarrassment.

Please don't laugh.
What is the level of discourse here?

To 'make out'. To go down on a man's penis. To lick a woman's anus. That is the level of discourse here. But I'm talking about loving a person's soul as revealed through their eyes. You have the eyes of the city. (*He runs his fingertips over her eyes and down her cheek.*) Please don't mention this to my wife.

Anne I don't *know* your wife.

Andrew Jennifer. Jennifer is my wife.

Anne I didn't know that.

Andrew You're not eating.

Anne I'm sorry?

Andrew You're not / eating.

Anne Is Jennifer your *wife*?

Andrew *Eat* something. Yes.

Anne How can you love me?

Andrew Look, dip this in the sauce. (*He demonstrates.*)

Anne How can you love me?

Andrew You're saying to yourself, 'I've known this man for only two hours.'

Anne Exactly.

Andrew You're saying, 'What has this got to do with my purpose in coming here?'

Anne Exactly.

Andrew You are beginning to doubt perhaps what that purpose is. That's a natural part of the process.

Anne What process?

A moment passes. Andrew dips food in the sauce and holds it up to her lips.

What process?

Andrew Eat.

Anne I'm not a child.

Andrew But you should eat.

Anne I'm not a child!

She knocks the chopsticks out of his hand.

(*quietly*) I don't want to be loved. That's not why I came.

She takes a cigarette. Andrew lights it.

Andrew You've come to us with your story.

Anne Exactly. *Yes.*

Andrew You've come to us with your story, but once you come to us with your story, your story is also ours. Because no one's story is theirs alone. I hope you realise that – Anne.

A moment passes. Jennifer appears and takes her place.

Jennifer Everybody happy?

She takes Anne's cigarette from her mouth and stubs it out.

Anne, you shouldn't smoke. You will die. D'you want to die?

All three laugh. Jennifer looks at her dish.

Is this what I ordered?

Andrew G. Yes.

Jennifer I ordered G? *Really?* (*to Anne*) No. I'm serious. D'you want to die?

Anne I had no idea you were Andrew's / wife.

Jennifer (*calls*) Excuse me. Waitress.
  Really? Does that surprise you? How long have we been married now?

Andrew Sixteen years.

Jennifer Who was that man in the street, Anne?

  Waitress appears. No pause.

Anne I'm sorry?

Jennifer (*to Andrew*) Sixteen? Is it? (*to Anne*) That man in the street. Who *was* that?

Andrew (*looking at Anne*) Of course she doesn't want to die. What kind of a question / is that?

Jennifer Was that the man you described? The engineer? Was that *him*?

Anne I'd never seen him / before.

Jennifer And yet he knew your name. He knew her name. He was calling / 'Anne'.

Andrew Anne is a common name.

Jennifer So is Jennifer. Anne is in fact less common *than* Jennifer, yet did he call 'Jennifer'? – no, he called 'Anne'.

Andrew He was drunk, Jen. He simply found Anne attractive and he called out (which is after all typical of a certain / kind of man).

Jennifer OK he found Anne attractive which she may well be but he still could've called 'Jennifer' – that's what I'm saying, Andrew. But in fact he called 'Anne' and Anne stopped –

Andrew Anne stopped because that is her name. Isn't that right, Anne?

Anne I just heard my name and stopped. / *Ob*viously.

Andrew And had he called 'Jennifer' then Jen would've stopped and we would be saying to Jen, 'Hey Jen, how come you are acquainted with that *ass*hole?'

Andrew and Anne both laugh but Jennifer continues over.

Jennifer This is not trivial, Andrew. Because the man called 'Anne' and Anne stopped and if this is the man of whom she was speaking then this disturbs me, this disturbs me because one I understood that on coming to us she had severed all links with this man because two what if this man wishes to exert a right a moral *right* over a story which after all is partly his and because three Anne from what you have said this is a dangerous a dangerous man (I mean the knife the tape the world the young trees *Je*sus.)

Waitress coughs.

(Yes, one moment.) So I'm asking you to confirm that that was not the man.

Andrew She says it's not the man.

Jennifer Anne?

,

Anne No.

Jennifer It wasn't.

Anne No. He was just a drunk.

,

Jennifer OK.

Anne I'd never seen him before.

Jennifer We won't pay you to lie to us, Anne.

Anne I would never *do* that.

Jennifer Well then that's fine. (*to waitress*) Yes, *I'm* sorry, you've just been standing there. I feel so awful because you may not believe this but I used to waitress and people treat you like / total shit, they really do. I mean Andrew

Andrew You really should eat something.

Anne I'm not hungry.

Jennifer remembers don't you Andy when I used to work in a place called *Corner Café* and the girls (I was a girl then) we all had to wear these aprons that said 'Meet me at the Corner'.

Andrew 'Meet me at the Corner.' That was a real humiliation.

Jennifer It's totally humiliating but the terrible thing Anne is that we accept these roles. 'Waitress', 'Customer', 'Victim', 'Oppressor'. Is this G?

Waitress G. Yes.

Jennifer Well I'm sorry, I wanted what he has, I wanted K.

Waitress You want K.

Jennifer If that's no trouble.

Waitress No trouble at all. (*She goes.*)

Jennifer And who was it said? because didn't somebody say that the ex-waitress is the shittiest customer and the ex-customer makes the most servile waitress. (*Laughs.*)

Yes that is profound, Anne, because it's true I treat these people like the scum of the earth.

Silence.

Anne So this is sushi.

Andrew This must be the moment she's always dreamed of.

Anne I'm not interested in dreams.

Jennifer We need something on paper, Anne. Did Andrew tell you? What has Andrew told you?

Anne Dreams are just circular.

Andrew Circular? Are they? How?

Anne In New York people dream of London, in London they dream of Paris, but in Paris they're dreaming of New York.

Jennifer We really do need something on paper, Anne. Did Andrew not say?

Anne (That's what I mean by circles.)

Andrew Uh-huh. That's interesting.

Jennifer Anne?

Anne Listen, I'm not a *writer*.

Jennifer Just something on paper. You don't have / to *write*.

Andrew We can *find* / a writer.

Jennifer Just tell the *paper* / what you've told *us*.

Anne Perhaps I need some time to think about this.

Jennifer Of course you do. Yes. Think. Just a page. That would be cool. Because we love your story. We want to be *part* / of it.

Andrew It's our story too.

Jennifer Exactly.

Anne OK.

Jennifer OK?

,

Anne (*softly*) He hated me even leaving the *house*. He'd bring the groceries back himself on the way home from work. He collected coupons. He was always so happy when he'd used coupons to buy an item. He used to say, 'Well Anne, look how much we've saved on this ten-ounce pack of freshly squeezed juice.' He tied me to the chair with pieces of wire. (*faint laugh*)

Jennifer Just a page, Anne.

Anne (*getting up*) I'm going to the Park. I need space to think.

Jennifer The Park is a good idea. Then come back to the office. *You* know where to find us.

As Anne moves away from the table Andrew follows her. At the same time waitress enters with K.

Is this K? You know, I don't think I'm hungry. I think we're going to leave. Oh *God* you come to a restaurant that's so *typical* no one wants to *eat*. (*She laughs.*)

Andrew (*sotto voce*) I *want* you, Anne.

Jennifer Could we just have the check, please.

4. Taxi!

Anne Taxi! Taxi!

The taxi driver appears.

Central Park West.

Driver Where *is* that?

Anne Where is what?

Driver Where do you want to go?

Anne Central Park. Central Park West.

Driver D'you know the way?

Anne Right. OK. Are you an immigrant?

Driver I've lived in this city all of my life.

Anne Uh-huh. My apologies.

Driver I know this city like the lines on my mother's face.

Anne OK. Just take me in that case just take me to Central Park West.

Driver I was born on a Hundred and Twenty-Ninth Street. I've lived in this city all of my life, I'm not an immigrant.

Anne I didn't mean to *offend* you.

Driver Am I offended?

Anne OK. I'm sorry. Let's just drive.

Driver Am I offended?

Anne Let's just drive.

Driver I picked you up on West Tenth – is that right?

Anne I guess.

Driver So I take a left here into Hudson, I pass Abingdon Square and I join Eighth Avenue. D'you see? It's simplicity.

Anne OK.

Driver Just tell me when we reach Abingdon.

Anne OK.

Driver I'd appreciate that.

'

Are you meeting someone in the Park?

Anne I'm sorry?

Driver Someone maybe that you love. Someone maybe whose hand you will hold, under the trees.

Anne I'm not meeting anybody. In fact I want I *need to* be on my own.

Blast of horn.

Anne OK so this is Abingdon. (Listen, you've just gone through a red / light.)

Driver Someone whose life maybe is dearer to you than your own.

'

Are we on Eighth?

Anne Yes. Just go straight uptown.

Driver Are you sure we're / on Eighth?

Anne I *know* we're on Eighth. (God the filth of this city how do we *live* like this look at that woman and her *child*. The garbage they are *eating* it no no no I can't / look.)

Driver Are you sure we're on Eighth?

Anne This is Eighth and Sixteenth. Yes. Just drive.

Driver And the light's green?

Anne You have a green light.

Driver Can you tell me if we come to another red?

Anne OK.

Driver I'd appreciate that.

Anne Well OK.

,

Can I ask you a question?

Driver I'm sorry?

Anne Can I ask you a question?

Driver What question is that?

Anne Do you have a visual problem? Is your sight impaired? Are you blind?

Driver I was *born* blind. Right up there on a Hundred and Twenty-Ninth Street. Today you would operate, but back then / nobody even knew

Anne (*intense panic*) *Oh* fuck. *Oh* Jesus Christ.

Driver it was a medical condition. Because I was born out of wedlock and my mother was just a child they thought this blindness was a judgement from *God*. / They thought

Anne Let me out.

Driver it was a *moral* issue not a health issue. Today it would take just a simple operation at birth but she was a poor woman and / she had *sinned*.

Anne STOP THE CAB! LET ME OUT OF THIS CAB!

Silence.
The taxi has stopped. Anne recovers her breath.
Very slowly the driver turns his face towards her.

Driver Is this where you want to get out?

,

Or drops. They just put drops in your eyes at birth.

Very slowly he turns back again.

You have to tell me the fare. That's the situation here.
One of trust. Some nights I have dreams about those
drops. I dream that I can see. I dream about light which
I have never seen.

Anne Just drive on.

Driver Don't you want to get out?

,

I thought you were *afraid*. I thought you wanted to / get
out.

Anne Just drive on to the Park.

5. TriBeCa. The Office.

Jennifer faces downstage, her mouth closed. Andrew sits
facing upstage in a chair, his back alone visible.

Andrew D'you feel confident in Anne? I feel confident in
Anne.

Jennifer empties the contents of her mouth into an
ashtray.

What do you think?

Jennifer About Anne?

Andrew stands, zips up his pants.

D'you think this is safe?

Andrew I think it's safe for *me*. (*faint laugh*)

Jennifer (*intercom*) Nicky?

Nicky's Voice Hello?

Jennifer (*intercom*) Could I have a glass of water, please.

Andrew (Not that I would endorse safety as a way of /
living.)

Jennifer I find her humourless.

Andrew Anne? Humourless?

Jennifer What did she say when you told her you loved
her?

Andrew That she didn't want to be loved.

Jennifer OK. But she believed you?

Andrew *Oh* yes.

Jennifer You looked into her eyes.

Andrew Yes.

Jennifer You said, 'I love you, Anne.'

Andrew Yes.

Jennifer And she believed you.

Andrew Yes.

*Both faint laugh. Nicky enters with a glass of water
and remains in the room.*

Jennifer It could be useful.

Andrew I think it *will be* useful. For her to feel as she now does that there is a commitment to her emotionally – / *personally.*

Jennifer But what do you really feel?

Andrew I'm sorry?

Jennifer What do you really feel about Anne?

Andrew What do I really / *feel?*

Jennifer You looked into her eyes.

Andrew Yes.

Jennifer You said, 'I love you, Anne.'

Andrew Yes.

Jennifer And she believed you.

,

Andrew Are you *jealous?*

Jennifer Nicky, is there something in particular you want?

Nicky Yes *I'm* sorry but you have Mr Webb waiting / to see you.

Andrew Are you *jealous?* Because these are only *words,* Jennifer.

Jennifer Webb?

Nicky He arrived just after one for his appointment at two. It's now four. I just thought I would – I mean he asked me / to mention –

Jennifer You say 'only words' but is it possible to use words without to some degree participating in their meaning? Because I'm not sure / that it is.

Andrew Perfectly possible. (*to Nicky*) Who is Webb?

Nicky He's a writer, Mr Wallace. He's been sitting out there for three hours.

Andrew You'd better show him in.

Nicky Shall I show him in?

Andrew I think you better had.

Nicky goes.

(Three hours, that's / criminal.)

Jennifer No Andrew, I am not 'jealous'. I'm simply questioning your level of insight.

Jennifer drinks the water as Nicky shows Webb in.

Nicky Mr Webb. (*She goes.*)

Clifford I'd rather you called me Clifford.

Andrew Clifford. Hello. Andrew.

They shake hands.

Jennifer Jennifer.

Clifford Pleased to meet you, Jennifer.

They shake hands. Clifford looks around.

Can I bum a cigarette from you?

Jennifer I'm sorry, / I don't smoke.

Andrew Absolutely. Here.

He gives Clifford a cigarette and lights it.

Clifford It's just I've been out there for a couple of (thank you) couple of hours and I got through my whole damn pack.

He inhales deeply. Jennifer and Andrew look at him in silence. He feels ill-at-ease and loosens his cravat.

June – it's so humid. In Washington Square people are just standing under the fountains, young men and women just standing there with their clothes stuck to their bodies.

He drags again on the cigarette.

There's a bench where I usually sit.

Andrew A bench.

Clifford In the shade.

Andrew Uh-huh.

,

Clifford Listen . . . it's very good of you both to give me so much of your time. It's appreciated. I mean I realise the script is . . .

Andrew Please. Sit down.

Clifford (*sitting*) I realise the script is (thank you) probably . . .

Andrew What script *is* that, Howard?

Clifford I'm sorry? I assumed that's what this / was about.

Andrew Do we have one of Howard's scripts?

Jennifer Is it a *format* or *treatment* or what is it exactly? / (I'm not sure.)

Clifford It's a drama.

Jennifer I'm sorry?

Clifford It's a drama. / I write comedy.

Jennifer Howard says it's a drama. I don't recall this material. D'you recall this material?

Andrew When did we receive it, Howard?

Jennifer (That's if we *have* / received it.)

Clifford About a year ago now.

Andrew OK.

Clifford You see six months of the year I do whatever is necessary / to live and for the other six months –

Andrew About a year ago. So that will mean that Nicky will've read it.

Jennifer Exactly. Nicky reads everything. She is *incredible*.

Andrew She will've written you see what she will've done is she will've written / a report.

Jennifer (*intercom*) Nicky, d'you have a report on / Howard's script?

Clifford Nicky. That's the girl on reception.

Andrew She's incredibly bright. She majored in Dance and Corporate Finance. She's here as an / intern.

Jennifer (*intercom*) OK could you make a copy and bring it in to us then.
  She remembers it clearly.
  She'll bring us a Xerox.

  Clifford has smoked his cigarette down to the butt.
  He goes to stub it out but hesitates on seeing the fluid
  in the ashtray. He drops the butt in.

Andrew *Tell* us something about yourself, Howard.

Clifford My name is Clifford.

Andrew *I'm* sorry.

,

Jennifer Clifford Webb.

Clifford You may know my name. A couple of my shows were big hits in the fifties. (Of course that's before you were even *born*.)

Jennifer That's very gallant of you, Clifford.

Andrew And what have you been doing / *since* then?

Jennifer Clifford is very / gallant.

Clifford And they were playing on Broadway – proper theatres – not these little holes that *call* / themselves theatres –

Andrew And what have you been doing *since* then?

Jennifer Clifford would probably like to know something about *us* – isn't that so? What would you like to know about *us*?

Andrew What *do* you know about us?

Clifford I've heard . . . very good things.

Jennifer (That's cool.)

Andrew OK well what we are is essentially we are *facilitators* meaning we are here because we wish to make connections we think of ourselves don't we Jen as a kind of chip, we're a chip and out there are many many inputs –

Jennifer Like the city itself.

Andrew Like the city itself exactly a *grid* into which things feed a grid yes or chip for which we the facilitators provide the logic the power while you provide people like yourself provide the input the signal –

Jennifer So this could be an idea / or a skill –

Andrew It could be an idea or a skill or often something less tangible

Nicky enters quietly and remains at the back of the room.

simply noise simply an input of noise pure noise something intangible yes and random which nevertheless comes on line it comes on line and generates the crucial transformation.

Jennifer The output.

Andrew The output. Exactly. Which is (we hope) / art.

Clifford Noise.

Andrew The kind of background you find (noise, yes) in a restaurant or a forest. Something which both is and is not silence.

,

(*Turns to Nicky.*) Nicky. Yes. (*She comes forward.*)

Jennifer Or it could be an image, Clifford. A woman's face, her eyes wide open in terror. Over her mouth a strip of reflecting tape. In the tape the image of her assailant's face forms and *re*-forms like globs of mercury.

Nicky I have the report, Mr Wallace.

Andrew Excellent. Read it to us.

Clifford *Read* it? Listen, don't you want to –

Andrew To what? To wait?

Jennifer Are you afraid? Don't be / afraid.

Andrew You've already waited three hours plus a year prior to that. I think we should just move on this. Nicky?

Nicky reads the report.

Nicky 'Clifford Webb. *The Tenant*. A drama.

Andrew offers Clifford a cigarette and lights it.

'A man in his sixties – Brooke – has spent a lifetime doing menial jobs in order to finance his secret life as a painter. He paints obsessively in a tenement building up in the hundreds, spending whatever he earns on paint and materials.

'He rarely goes out, but one night he ventures into an East Village bar where he gets into a conversation with a young couple. They are art dealers and amuse themselves by getting Brooke drunk. However they miscalculate, and after a few hours become drunk themselves.

'When the couple say they must leave, Brooke asks to come with them. The man, Ethan, objects to this but is over-ruled by Clara, the girl.

'In their apartment on Christopher they continue to drink with Brooke until – it's not quite clear how this comes about, does Brooke suggest it, or does he merely amplify a hint of Clara's? – it is agreed that Brooke will watch Ethan and Clara make love.

'This he does from a wicker chair at the foot of their bed.

'Tacitly – that is with no spoken agreement – this arrangement continues night after night until Brooke becomes part of the household.

'He abandons his casual work and begins instead to cook and clean for the couple, as well as caring for their baby son. In return he is allowed to be spectator of their most intimate moments.

'One afternoon, driving across town, Brooke is killed in a collision with a fire-truck.

'From this point on we witness the progressive degeneration of the young couple's relationship. Without the gaze of Brooke they no longer have any desire for each other. And in the absence of desire it soon becomes clear they have no other bond. Ethan immerses himself in his work at the gallery for longer and longer periods until Clara, disillusioned with a world which seems preoccupied only with fragments and surfaces, finally takes their son and joins the Amish.

'Several months later the new tenant of Brooke's apartment discovers a concealed doorway. She calls in a locksmith. The door leads to a basement beneath the stoop of the tenement. Inside are a number of paintings.

'These are the paintings made by Brooke during the last weeks of his life. They depict Clara and Ethan and are a unique record of the beauty of the human form at its most vulnerable. They are the work of a master at the height of his powers.

'The new tenant however considers the pictures obscene. With a pocket knife she cuts the canvases from the stretchers and burns them.'

Silence.

Andrew (*softly*) It's a mindfuck, Clifford.

Jennifer This is a total mindfuck. Why haven't we seen this, Nicky?
(*to Andrew*) Have *you* seen this?

Andrew *I've* never seen this.

Jennifer Nicky?

,

Andrew (*shakes Clifford's hand*) Congratulations.

Clifford Thank you.

Jennifer (*to Nicky*) Well?

Nicky I *tried* to show you this.

Jennifer I don't recall.

Simultaneous conversations:

Nicky I tried to show you this but you said not to waste my time with un- solicited / material.

Andrew You told us you wrote *comedies*.

Clifford There *are* some funny lines.

Jennifer I don't *believe* that.

Andrew She burns the paintings. That is a *mind*fuck. You are a dark horse, Clifford.

Nicky You said why was I reading it. It should be *shredded*.

Jennifer Shredded? I never said 'shredded'. Are you trying to *embarrass* me?

Clifford I've used a lot of personal experience. *Feelings*.

Nicky *I'm* sorry.

Andrew Of *course* you have.

Jennifer I never said 'shredded' Nicky. I have great respect for people's endeavours. *You* know that. It's a *privilege* to see people's work. If I said 'shredded' I was kidding you.

Clifford There's a sense in which *I* am *Brooke*.

Andrew It's a metaphor.

Clifford In a way.

Andrew And it's so *real*.

Clifford So d'you think this can be used?

Nicky OK.

Jennifer OK?

Andrew Used? Of course it can be used. We would be *privileged* to use this.

Clifford For many years I've despaired. I'll be frank.

'

If something like this comes along I want it on my *desk*.

Andrew Don't despair.

Clifford This is the moment I've always dreamed of.

Nicky It was *on* your desk.

It was on your desk for two weeks.

Jennifer I don't want to argue.

Nicky Then I filed it.

Jennifer I'm not arguing with you.

,

Andrew Of *course* it is.

Clifford Look at me. I'm *shaking*.

Andrew Have a cigarette.

Clifford Thank you.

Andrew Listen. I have an idea. There's someone you should meet. You should meet Anne.

Clifford Who is Anne?

Andrew Don't you think, Jen? He should meet Anne?

What?
  (*to Nicky*) You can go.

  Nicky goes.

What?

Andrew I think Clifford should meet Anne.

Jennifer Who is Anne?

Andrew *Our* Anne. Don't you think?

,

Clifford Who is Anne?

Jennifer Anne. *Yes.*

  Blackout.

Act Two

1. Central Park.

Anne lies on the grass with a blank sheet of paper. She pays no attention to two movie stars playing from Act Five, Scene Two of Othello, *their voices amplified by throat mikes.*

Movie Star 1 (*as Othello*)
He, woman:
I say thy husband; dost understand the word?
My friend, thy husband – honest, honest Iago.

Movie Star 2 (*as Emilia*)
If he say so, may his pernicious soul
Rot half a grain a day! He lies to th' heart.
She was too fond of her most filthy bargain.

Movie Star 1
Ha!

Movie Star 2
Do thy worst:
This deed of thine is no more worthy heaven
Than thou wast worthy her.

Movie Star 1
Peace, you were best.

Movie Star 2
Thou hast not half that power to do me harm
As I have to be hurt. O gull! O dolt!
As ignorant as dirt! Thou hast done a deed –
I care not for thy sword; I'll make thee known,

Though I lost twenty lives. Help! help, ho! help!
The Moor hath kill'd my mistress! Murder! Murder!

*During the preceding speech Simon enters, unseen by
Anne. The movie stars disappear. We become aware of
the long evening shadows.*

Simon watches Anne for a long time before speaking.

Simon (*softly*) Anne?

Anne is startled but turns to him slowly.

You look different.
Have you changed your hair?
What have you changed?

Anne Nothing.

,

Simon takes her sheet of paper and holds it up.

Simon What's this?

Anne What does it look like?

*Anne tries to recover the paper but he lifts it out of
her reach and folds it as he speaks.*

Simon I think it is your letter of reconciliation. I think
you're trying to find words to express your sorrow and
shame.

Anne I have nothing to be ashamed of.

Simon Everyone misses you.

Anne Who is everyone?

Simon They ask after you.

Anne I don't know them.

Simon They're *concerned* for you.

Anne I don't know them, Simon.

,

Simon Your hair used to be brown. Your eyes were blue.

Anne My eyes *are* blue.

Simon But not the blue they used to be, Anne.

He's made a paper flower. He gives it to her.

How are you living? You can't shop. You can't cook.

Anne They gave me an advance. They checked me into a hotel. I don't *need* to cook, Simon.

Simon Which hotel?

,

I hate Shakespeare in the Park. It pollutes the Park.

Anne (*without interest*) Does it?

Simon Didn't you see it?

Anne When I snap my fingers you're going to disappear.

Simon I don't think so.

Anne You're going to disappear, Simon.

She snaps her fingers and begins to turn away. However, he grasps her wrist.

Simon What do they want from you?

Anne Nothing. Ideas. Let go of me.

Simon What ideas? What ideas do you have?

Anne They want me to tell my story. It's nothing.

Simon You don't have a story. What story?

He's hurting her.

What story?

Anne Nothing, Simon. Just –

Simon What?

Anne Whatever I can recall. Childhood. That kind of shit like being swung up into the air by your father and screaming and screaming or being knocked down by the ocean for the first time when the salt water gets somewhere behind your mouth your nose you don't know where the water is you think you're going to die LET GO OF ME!

Simon Childhood?

He releases her. Anne rubs her wrist and begins to laugh.

Anne You know what they tried to make me eat today. Raw fish.

Simon Raw fish. That's degrading.

They both laugh.

(*gently*) Come back with me.

Anne It's Japanese.

Simon Come back, Anne. They'll corrupt you.

Anne He tried to feed me with it. (*She laughs.*)

Simon 'He'?

Anne Yes.

Simon Who is 'he'? Is he the man?

Anne Of course 'he' is the man. What else / could he be?

Simon You looked right through me in the street. I felt transparent.

Anne Did I?

Simon He tried to feed you. Where?

Anne In my mouth.

Simon Obviously in your mouth.

,

Obviously in your mouth, Anne.

Anne *He* mentioned my eyes.

She turns away and unfolds the flower, smoothing out the paper, smiling to herself.

I'm not coming back, Simon. I'm never coming back. I have my own room. Money. People who are (because they *are*) *interested* in me.

Simon Interested in corrupting you . . .

Anne Well perhaps I want to be corrupted. Perhaps I *need* to be corrupted. I've spent my life with you behind a *steel door.*

Simon . . . people who feed you in the mouth, who give you money to tell them what happened to you as a *child* –

Anne Not just as a child, Simon. They want to hear about us. They want to hear about you. (*faint laugh*)

The distant sound of applause and cries of 'Bravo!' from Othello.

Touch me and I'll scream.

She stands her ground smiling faintly at Simon.
The applause and cries grow louder, carried on the wind.

2. The Japanese Restaurant.

Jennifer and Clifford eat with the movie star who played Othello. His name is John. The waitress attends them. John's manner is notably measured and relaxed.

John Damaged in what way?

Jennifer I would say socially, wouldn't you, Clifford.

John Because I am wary of the equation 'black equals damaged'. I'm sure you understand that. I am wary of the equation 'black equals street'.

Jennifer Exactly but this is not a street guy. This man is educated. He's a – what is he, Clifford?

Clifford An engineer.

Jennifer He's an electrical engineer.

John Uh-huh.

Jennifer And what distinguishes him – as I was trying to explain – is that he has a vision.

John OK. That's good. Vision is good.

Jennifer So when we say 'damaged', John, we're talking essentially we're talking about a man who is *outside* of the society in which he finds himself –

Clifford Marginalised.

Jennifer And when we saw your Othello (marginalised, exactly) your Othello tonight in the Park . . .

Clifford (*to waitress*) A little more champagne, please.

Jennifer . . . it blew my mind away . . .

John Thank you.

Jennifer . . . it blew my mind away because – well because the parallels are so striking, and I immediately knew you would be so *right* for this.

Clifford I'd like to introduce a Shakespearean element.

He drinks greedily. The waitress goes.

John You are the writer.

Jennifer Clifford has only just come on board.

John I'm sorry, I don't know your work.

Jennifer And what is exciting is that this is a true story over which we have complete control.

John nods, reflects.

John Jennifer and I go back a long time, Clifford, a long long time. I remember her with hair down to her waist and bells round her ankles, don't I Jen. *(faint laugh)* Look at her. She's embarrassed. But why?

I can remember her lying down in the street to protest. I remember because I lay beside her, Clifford. That's how far back we go. Side by side. In the street.

We felt that our actions might transform the world. We felt that if our own relationships were free of the tensions of race, sex, money, then the world itself would alter. In the way that if you begin to grow plants in a stagnant pool, over time the body of water will become clear. *(He laughs at the naivety of this idea.)* We saw this happening not for ourselves, but perhaps for our children. Not that we had children, Clifford. Since as I'm sure you realise, it's one thing to hang out with a black man, but something else again to marry him, to have his children.

Jennifer looks away. John is amused by her embarrassment, but not bitter.

Jennifer (I'm sure Clifford doesn't want to hear about our wasted / youth, John.)

John And if I didn't still possess such a strong picture of the girl who lay down beside me to protest about something I have entirely forgotten, then I would not – Clifford – contemplate getting involved even for one moment in the kind of degrading shit that has become her trademark.

A moment, before John begins to laugh.

Come on, Jen. A joke.

Jennifer joins in the laughter a little uncertainly. John lays his hand on the back of Clifford's neck – a good-humoured gesture which nevertheless disturbs Clifford.

A writer. A man of principle.

He continues to laugh as Clifford tries to move out of his grip. The waitress reappears.

Waitress I have a call for a Mr Webb? Clifford Webb?

Clifford Excuse me.

Clifford disengages himself and goes with the waitress. John watches him go, laughing and shaking his head.

John 'Shakespearean element.' He kills me.

Silence.

Jennifer I resent your description of our work, John.

John How is Andrew?

Jennifer What you said was not true.

John simply laughs and makes a gesture of mock surrender.

John How is Andrew?

Jennifer He's fine.

John I hear interesting things.

Jennifer About Andrew?

John About both of you. Very interesting things.

Jennifer You've always been unbearable when you moralise.

John Moralise?

Again he laughs and repeats 'surrender' gesture.

A man in a hood.
He's damaged.
He's black.
He ties women up with pieces of wire.
He forces them to touch him.
He abuses them.
But he has a vision.

John laughs and shakes his head, apparently in utter disbelief, before becoming serious:

I would want veto of cast.
I would want writer-approval.
I would require producer-credit.
I would require complete control.
Think about it.

He begins to laugh again. Clifford reappears, smoking.

You know something, Jennifer. You're still beautiful. You haven't changed. Don't you find this woman beautiful, Clifford.

Jennifer Is something wrong?

Clifford I have to go.

Jennifer Are you going?

Without sitting, Clifford drains his glass of champagne.

John There's a kind of beauty that survives. *I* don't possess it.

Jennifer Are you alright?

Clifford I must go. I need to work

John It's been a pleasure, Clifford.

John shakes Clifford's hand. Clifford goes.

'I must go.' 'I must work.'

He laughs.

3. Upper West Side. Andrew and Jennifer's Apartment.

A chair. An ambiguous sofa/bed.
A uniformed maid lights candles. Anne sits on the edge of the sofa examining a gun.

Anne Who does this gun belong to?

The maid says nothing.

I hate weapons.

The maid says nothing.

I nearly *sat* on it. Shouldn't it be put away somewhere?

Andrew enters, unseen by Anne.

I said: shouldn't this be *put* somewhere?

Andrew She doesn't speak English.

Anne I nearly *sat* on this. Is it yours? I hate weapons.

Andrew (*taking the gun*) It's Jennifer's. I'm sorry.

Anne What does she want with a gun? (*faint laugh*)

Andrew (*shrugs*) Sometimes she feels threatened, that's all.

> Andrew puts the gun away. He tells the maid that she can go. She wishes them goodnight and withdraws.

Anne Is that Italian?

Andrew Spanish.

> Silence.

Anne I've brought the page.

Andrew What page is that? The *page*?

Anne The page. *This* page.

> She passes him the page. He glances through it.

Anne Jennifer said she wanted it.

Andrew Uh-huh. 'Jennifer said.'

'

Anne Is that the kind of thing you mean?

> Andrew looks up from the page and stares at her. He screws up the page and tosses it away.

Andrew Why did you come here?

Anne To bring you the page. Jennifer said –

Andrew 'Jennifer said.' Is Jennifer *here*?

Anne I don't know.

Andrew She's not. She's not here. She's out of town.

Silence.
   Anne gets up to retrieve the page.

Anne I'm sorry. I'll just / go.

Andrew Please don't go. (*He goes up to her. He takes the paper gently from her hand.*) We don't need this, that's all.

,

Drink?

Anne I lied to you.

Andrew Oh?

Anne It *was* my husband. The man who called out to me. And again tonight in the Park.

Andrew In the Park. Really? Your husband.

Anne Yes.

Andrew Tonight? What did he say to you?

Anne He asked me to come back.

Andrew To your Avenue.

Anne To Avenue X, yes. (*faint laugh*) He said I'd be corrupted.

Andrew And what did you say to that? To what extent did he mean 'corrupted'? (*He hands her a drink.*)

,

Anne It's just that Jennifer said –

Andrew 'Jennifer said.'

   He laughs and this time she joins in and relaxes. She sips the drink and looks round the room.

330

Anne If he could see me here he would / kill me.

Andrew Jennifer tends to over-react. She panics. Now I'm the opposite (if you can have an opposite of over / react.)

Anne You *under*-react.

Andrew Exactly.

They both laugh.

Anne You under-react because you have no feelings. You are emotionally dead.

She laughs.

The eyes of the city. What did you mean?

She drinks. Silence.

It's so hot in my hotel room I take endless showers. There's no bathroom *in* the room so I have to cross the corridor to the shower. The curtain is rotting especially at the bottom where it's permanently damp there's a kind of black mould growing on the blue plastic and people've left scraps of soap which I use to wash because I'm permanently scattered in this heat and I forget my own. So I take a shower with the scraps of soap then it's back to my room. I throw myself down on the bed and just lie there drying off in the current of air from the fan which I keep on maximum. For the first time in my life, my whole life, I'm completely free and alone and I can't bear it.

She drinks.

I've never travelled out of this *state* and yet I think I must be somehow jetlagged because I can't sleep but I can't really wake up – is that what it's like? I just go from the shower to the bed and back to the shower again and my

thoughts are in a loop: how I replied to the ad never
thinking anything would happen – then there was the
call and the limo arrived – it was so *long* and white and
cool inside and the driver never met my eyes – then you
listened to my story and we went to the restaurant where
I must've made such a fool of myself knowing nothing
about anything, what to *order*, how to use *chopsticks*,
nothing, what to *say* to you, and I reply to the ad and
the call comes, and the limo comes, and I tell my story,
and we go to the restaurant and I just lie there staring
at the fan which is like a person a disapproving person
shaking its head going 'no no no I don't believe this can
be you Anne no no no no no no no . . .'

As she chants 'no no no . . .' she moves her head
slowly from side to side in imitation of the fan, her
eyes shut. Andrew comes behind her and gently takes
hold of her head, stilling it.

Andrew We could change your hotel.

She opens her eyes. She moves away, sipping the
drink.

Anne I've escaped from the man who silenced and
humiliated me. So why does it feel like I'm betraying
him?

Andrew We could change your hotel. You shouldn't be
in that kind of hotel. Does *he* know where you're
staying?

Anne All the scraps of soap. I must smell of so many
different people . . .

Andrew Does *he* know where you're staying? Might he
harm you?

Anne Simon?

Andrew Might he? You said if he found you here he would kill you.

Anne That's just a figure of speech.

Andrew OK. Good.

Anne Because he wouldn't kill me, obviously. What he would do is kill *you*. That would be the most likely thing. Because he *can be* violent (did I not say how violent he can be?).

Andrew Simon.

Anne He wants to protect me, yes. (*faint laugh*)

Did I not say? He'd love this room. The furniture. The light.

Andrew Are you saying he's killed?

Anne Well hasn't everyone in this city? (Either killed or *been* killed . . .) (*She laughs. She's drinking too much.*) I thought that was what excited you. The 'present'. The 'moment'.

Andrew You couldn't begin to imagine what excites me – Anne.

Anne Really?

> *For the first time Anne is a little afraid.*
> *Faint knocking.*
> *Knocking a second time.*
> *Andrew turns to the door.*

Andrew Yes? Hello?

> *Knocking again.*

Excuse me.

333

*Andrew goes to the door and slips out leaving Anne
alone. She swallows the remains of the drink and puts
the glass down beside the crumpled page which she
opens out.*

*She lies stomach-down on the ambiguous sofa and
reads the page to herself, mumbling the words aloud
in such a way that they are not intelligible.
Occasionally she laughs softly at what she reads.
During this, Andrew reappears at the door.*

*He watches Anne, unseen by her, as she mumbles
and laughs. Eventually she senses his presence and
falls silent without looking at him.*

Corruption, Anne, has three stations. The first is the loss
of innocence. The second is the desire to inflict that loss
on others. The third is the need to instil in others that
same desire.

Anne (*turning to him*) Which station are we at?

Andrew shuts the door.

*He approaches Anne who moves onto her back. She
expects and is willing to have intercourse with him –
but not at all prepared for the sudden brutality of it.*

*Andrew penetrates her without any preliminaries.
He comes immediately, immediately lifts himself
away and drops onto his back.*

*Clifford appears in the room – not through the
door, but from where he's been standing in the
shadows. He drags on a cigarette.*

Andrew You're a dark horse, Clifford.

Anne (*sits up*) Who is that? Get him out. Was he
watching us? (*She gets up.*)

Andrew I'd like you to meet Clifford.

Clifford This may not be the moment.

Andrew Clifford is your writer.

Anne Was he *watching* us? Get him the fuck out of here.

Clifford This may not be the moment. I understand.

Anne Get out.

Clifford I understand.

'

No. Really. / I do.

Anne A *writer*?

Clifford A couple of shows of mine were big hits in the fifties. Of course that's before you / were even born.

Anne (*to Andrew*) I thought we were alone.

Andrew We are alone, Anne.

Clifford I'm very interested / in your story.

Andrew He's very interested in your story. He just wanted to try something, to *experience* something / that's all.

Anne (*approaching Clifford*) To try something.

Clifford Yes.

Anne And now you've – what? – you've tried it.

Clifford Yes.

Anne So how was it?

Clifford Listen I understand exactly what you must feel at this moment.

'

Anne So what do I feel? Tell me – I'm interested – what I feel.

'

335

Andrew Anne . . .

Anne spits in Clifford's face.

Anne That's what I feel.

,

Clifford I respect that.

Anne That's what I *feel*.

Andrew Clifford's an old man and also a very good writer. You don't have to spit on him. Jesus.

Anne I hope you *die*, Clifford. I hope you *burn*.

For a moment Anne stands paralysed by anger and humiliation. Then she walks out, pushing past Jennifer who has just appeared in the doorway.

Jennifer (*calls after her*) Anne? Anne?

,

Clifford Listen, if I've offended anyone . . .

Jennifer You're an artist, Clifford. It's your job to give offence. (*Calls again.*) Anne?

,

Oh god oh god I feel I've missed something. Have I missed something? Because there is a charge in the air, like when you rub fur on a stick.

,

Andrew How was your meal?

Jennifer We made progress. Only Clifford deserted us.

Andrew He had to work.

Jennifer I know (*She smiles at Clifford.*) We all have to work. (*She sees Anne's page where it's fallen on the floor. She picks it up.*)

Jennifer What's this?

Andrew Her story.

Blackout.

Act Three

1. TriBeCa. The Office.

Jennifer, Andrew, John, Nicky, Clifford.
  Boogie-woogie music.
  John dances with Nicky, Jennifer with Clifford.
Andrew sits watching them, without pleasure.
  At a solo break in the music it transpires that Nicky (and John ideally) is an extraordinary dancer.
  Jennifer and Clifford stand aside, clicking their fingers and shouting approval as Nicky and John do their stuff.
  Andrew takes no part in this. He is the first to notice that Anne has appeared in the doorway and is watching the dance.
  He turns off the music. The dance stops.
  Silence.
  Anne's appearance has changed. Her hair is fashionably cropped. She wears a very plain very expensive dress. She takes off her dark glasses revealing eyes darkened by sleeplessness. She looks unwell. John is first to speak.

John This must be Anne.

Jennifer You look different . . .

Anne I changed my hotel.

Jennifer . . . it suits you.

      ,

Anne Am I late?

John We were just dancing. D'you dance? Are you a dancer?

338

Jennifer This is John.

Anne John. OK.

John Very pleased to meet you.

He shakes her hand. Jennifer continues the formalities.

Jennifer Nicky you know.

Anne and Nicky acknowledge each other.

Clifford you've met.

Clifford nods and smiles. Anne simply stares at him. It grows awkward.

Let's take five minutes everyone.

Three conversations A, B and C now occur simultaneously. A finishes first, then B, and finally Anne and Andrew in C.

A

Jennifer John, you wanted to speak with me . . .

John It's a small matter but I feel we should resolve it now.

Jennifer Tell me what's on your mind. (*Cue Nicky in B.*)

John It's a question basically it's a question of personnel.

Jennifer's attention is on Andrew and Anne.

The creep has got to go.

Jennifer What creep? You say 'creep' – the world is full of creeps, John.

John You know the creep I mean.

Jennifer follows John's glance.

339

Jennifer Clifford?

John Uh-huh.

Jennifer But Nicky likes his work. She says he is / a great craftsman.

John Nicky is an intellectual, Jen. The qualities she admires are precisely the ones we need to lose. I would find it impossible to work with him.

Jennifer So Clifford is out.

,

Will *you* tell him?

John I'm happy to tell him. Is there a contract?

Jennifer Are you kidding?

John Then the matter is resolved.

They fall silent as they watch Andrew and Anne.

B

Nicky is left with Clifford. A moment's unease between them before Nicky speaks – cue 'Tell me what's on your mind' in A.

Nicky You're so like my grandfather. Of course *he's* dead. (*Cue Andrew in* C.) My grandmother moved to Sun City. She's considering cryotherapy.

Clifford Cryotherapy.

Nicky Yes, it's a process whereby your body is preserved after death in liquid nitrogen at or close to absolute zero.

340

Clifford I like to think my *work* will outlive me.

,

Nicky I write a little myself.

Clifford Really? That's interesting.

Nicky Yes I've published one or two novels and I also write in a small way for the theatre.

Clifford Uh-huh?

Nicky I guess I've just been very lucky because some people struggle for years and of course I've never suffered in the way you must've done (except when my parents divorced, *that* was hard).

Clifford (Did they?)

Nicky (My dad had an alcohol problem. Yes.)

They fall silent as they watch Andrew and Anne.

C

As Jennifer begins to speak to John, Andrew takes Anne's arm and leads her downstage. Andrew's cue to speak is Nicky's 'Of course he's dead' in B.

Andrew (*with quiet concern*) You look terrible, Anne. Has something happened?

Anne I'm not sleeping.

,

Andrew Why didn't you return my calls?

Anne What calls?

Andrew I kept calling you. I've needed to speak to you.

341

He touches her cheek. She flinches.

I've wronged you.

Anne I hate that man.

Andrew What man, Anne? Your husband?

Anne That man. The writer.

Andrew It was a mistake. Please. Trust me.

Anne I can't sleep thinking about it.

Andrew Trust me, Anne.

Anne About him.

,

Andrew I've wronged you. (*He takes her hand.*)

Anne How can I believe anything you say to me?

,

Have you really tried to call me?

Andrew Every day. I sent you *flowers*.

Anne Were those from you?

Andrew Wasn't there a card?

Anne I didn't look.

Andrew Didn't you look?

Anne The flowers were beautiful.

Andrew Didn't you look at the card? Of course they were from me.

,

Anne (*faint laugh*) I've never seen so many *colours*.

Andrew Didn't you look at the card? I want us to start over, Anne. I want you to come away with me.

Silence. Andrew realises that the others have become aware of the intimacy of their conversation.

I'll speak to you / later.

Jennifer (*claps hands*) OK can we begin everybody. Andrew. Anne. Clifford. Nicky – would you like to stay? Anne? You have no objection to Nicky staying? I feel she should be involved.

Anne shakes her head: no objection.
Andrew lights a cigarette for her.
Slight adjustments to positioning.
All wait for Anne to speak.

Anne Could I have a glass of water?

Andrew goes out to get it.
All wait again.
Andrew returns, gives water to Anne, and sits beside her again.

Jennifer OK. We're in your apartment. It's seven p.m. He's brought some stuff home and fixed you a meal. Let's say: spaghetti.

Laughter from John, Nicky, Clifford.

You've been chatting about this and that. And now he comes over to you. Is that right?

Anne That's right. He comes over to me.

Jennifer He comes over to you and he sticks tape over your mouth.

Anne Yes.

Jennifer Why?

Anne To silence me. He wants to silence me. We've been / through this.

John That's very strange. Why does he want to silence you, Anne?

Anne Uh . . .

John Is it the sound, the *sound* of your voice, the timbre maybe of your voice?

Anne I'm sorry?

Jennifer Is it the voice, Anne, or what the voice is saying?

Anne I guess it's what I'm saying.

John What are you saying?

Anne He finds me critical.

John Of what? Of him? You're critical of him? Why?

Nicky (Isn't that obvious?)

Anne Not of him.

John (Not necessarily.)

Anne Not of him. No. More generally critical I mean this is of the neighbourhood. Because he was brought up there and to him it's home, he just doesn't see the violence or the dirt, he feels I / exaggerate.

John What d'you mean 'brought up there'?

Anne Well his grandfather managed freaks on Coney Island in its heyday and his mother and father still run a bar down there to this day – 'The Lucky Throw' – you may / know it.

John Because I don't see him, Jen, as having this kind of background at all.

Jennifer We'll come back to that / John.

Anne In fact on our first date he took me on the Cyclone – you know, the old roller-coaster down there – afterwards he said, 'I've never heard anyone scream so much' (which was strange you know because I had no recollection of screaming I must've been / so *out* of it).

John I don't see him as having this kind of background. Freaks. Bar-tender. No way.

Anne What d'you mean?

'

What does he mean?

Jennifer Tell us about the tape.

Anne No. What does he mean?

Jennifer These are just possible changes, Anne.

Anne What 'changes'? (*to Andrew*) What does she mean?

Jennifer John is attracting a great deal of money to this.

Anne I don't want anything changed.

Jennifer A great deal of money, Anne. Your new hotel. Your / *clothes*.

John Perhaps 'changes' is too strong a word. It's more a question of where we place the emphasis.

Anne (*warily*) OK.

John OK?

'

Jennifer Tell John about the tape.

Anne I explained all this before.

345

Jennifer John would like to hear.

Anne Well he always has this tape on account of his job. (He's an engineer. He installs telephones.)

John Is that a skilled job?

Anne I'm sorry, I've no idea. I really don't see that / it matters.

John Is he educated? Did he study?

Jennifer No, I think John's right to be concerned.

John Did he?

Anne I think he studied for a while. Then he became disillusioned. (I don't really know the / details.)

John (*to Jennifer*) Disillusion is good. I can do something with that.

Nicky Tell me something: do you struggle?

  ,

Anne I'm sorry?

Jennifer (Disillusion. OK.)

Nicky Do you struggle?

Anne *Inwardly* I struggle, but –

Nicky But not physically. Why is that?

Anne What point would there be? He's much stronger than I am and at least this way I know I won't be hurt.

Nicky Because I think there must be a struggle. Are we saying she just sits there and lets the guy do this. I find that unbelievable. And besides I object very strongly to the idea of woman as victim, woman as dead meat.

Anne I'm not a victim. Dead meat? What is she / *talking* about.

Nicky (*to John*) I think that kind of passivity is / totally degrading

John I agree. It's / unacceptable.

Anne I'm not a victim. Fuck *you*.

Nicky 'Not a victim.' *That's* cool. (Of course / she's a victim.)

Jennifer Nicky, can you / ease up.

Nicky *I* say she struggles. *I* say she resists. I say how can she *tolerate* this treatment from a man?

John So it becomes violent.

Nicky Of *course* it becomes violent.

Anne She knows nothing about this. Can't somebody / explain –

Nicky You see: (*indicating Anne*) this is not my idea of Anne.

John Now that's *very* interesting.

Anne Listen to me, this is my story, I've *lived* this.

Nicky This is not my idea of Anne: passive? humiliated? victim? – She's 'lived' it. Haven't we also lived?

Jennifer Nicky, you have no / right to –

John Please. Let her speak.

Nicky You've 'lived' it. OK. But what does that mean? What if what you've lived is in fact banal? Must we accept that? No. We have a duty not to accept that, Anne, a duty to ourselves, a duty / to *you*.

John I think Brooke is the key to this.

Nicky I think Brooke could well be – yes – / the key.

John Tell us something about Brooke.

Anne Who is Brooke?

Clifford Brooke is the old man who watches you both.

Anne Excuse me?

Jennifer (*to John*) Brooke is Clifford's idea, John. / He's not –

John (*to Anne*) He interests me. What's his background?

Clifford He does menial work but has a secret life as an artist. / Every day he –

John I'd rather hear it from Anne, Clifford. Anne?

Anne What?

John Tell us about Brooke.

Andrew She doesn't *know* about Brooke.

Jennifer Clifford wants to introduce a voyeuristic / element.

John (*to Jennifer*) Why doesn't she know about Brooke?

Andrew Brooke isn't real. *Wait* / a minute.

John Isn't real? You mean she imagines him? I don't / buy that.

Anne I don't know who / Brooke is.

John I don't buy that. He has to be real. He has to be *there*, in the apartment. (*to Nicky*) Isn't that right? He's there?

Nicky Absolutely. He's right there. He witnesses / their sexual acts.

John He witnesses – exactly, thankyou – their sexual / acts.

Anne (*increasingly distressed*) What sexual acts? There are no sexual acts. There is no struggle. There is no other person. Just Simon and myself. I've told you this. He doesn't touch me, he talks to me. (*to Andrew*) Why are they changing / everything?

John Of course he talks, Anne. People talk. Which is why we require dialogue. But the talking is only the build. He has a vision – accepted – but that is only the build. (*to Jennifer*) Incidentally I'm not happy with this 'secret life' idea.

Clifford I'm sorry but who exactly is writing this?

Jennifer (We have to talk, / Clifford.)

John We must have a release, Anne.

Anne But he doesn't touch me . . . He's *never* touched me . . .

John A release.

Anne He's not interested in that aspect of marriage . . .

John Now in this case the release is a sexual act –

Nicky Series would be better.

John Series would indeed be better of acts witnessed by a third person, Brooke. (*to Jennifer*) I thought we'd discussed this.

Anne Not with me. NOT / WITH ME. (*She weeps.*)

John Because your life is interesting, Anne . . .

Nicky Absolutely.

John Undoubtedly interesting – up to a point. We are here to help you get beyond that point.

349

Anne continues to weep from exhaustion and strain.
A moment passes.

Andrew (*softly but firmly*) She's saying he only talks.

John Are you *defending* her?

Anne begins to moan.

Clifford What is it you have to say to me?

Jennifer This isn't the moment, Clifford.

Anne continues to moan – a thin monotone.

Let's give her some space everybody.
Anne, would you like some space?

Anne doesn't speak. She seems oblivious.

Andrew, Clifford, Nicky – John – I'm sorry – would you mind very much leaving the room so Anne and I can have some space?

They do so. As they go John puts his arm around Clifford.

John Jennifer has asked me to clarify the situation, Clifford.

Clifford Uh-huh? What situation is that?

John Exactly. It needs to be clarified . . . (*faint laugh*)

They go out. Andrew is last to leave, glancing back as he goes.
Anne remains moaning. Jennifer comes downstage to where she sits. She moves the glass of water out of the way, then strikes Anne's face with such force that she falls to the floor.

Jennifer You offend *John*.
You fuck *my* husband in *my* apartment.

Anne huddles on the floor.

Anne (*incoherent*) I was lonely.

Jennifer What?

,

WHAT?

Anne I WAS LONELY.

Jennifer You were lonely. Couldn't you just talk?

,

I don't know what to do, Anne. You seem to have taken everything and given nothing.

Anne begins to whine unintelligibly. Jennifer looks on.

I can't hear what you're saying. (God, I wish I smoked.)

Andrew slips into the room.

I can't hear what she's saying.

,

Andrew Why is she on the floor?

,

Jennifer (*shrugs*) Perhaps you can communicate with her.

Jennifer goes out. Andrew remains at a distance from Anne who has completely surrendered to her need to weep and keen. He lights a cigarette.

Andrew I'm forty-four years old, Anne, but I sit at my desk and I write your name on pieces of paper. A-n-n-e. Anne. Then I strike it out in embarrassment. When I told you I loved you I thought, 'OK this will be useful, I'll have some control,' but now I find I meant what I said. The words, just the words, brought the emotion into being, and look at me – I have no control at all.

Is it because you're real? We don't often meet real people here. We ourselves have no memories or stories. No enchantment, Anne. We are the disenchanted. We started out real, but the real-ness has burned out of us.

Anne pays no attention. She remains huddled. Andrew crouches beside her and raises her head by the hair, forcing her eyes to meet his.

Come away with me. Now.

Anne (*with effort*) I don't . . . want . . . to be loved.

There's a commotion outside. Andrew roughly releases his grip. Clifford barges in, followed by John who is trying to hold him back.

Clifford This nigger tells me I'm fired. What right does he have?

John (*gripping him*) Ease up, my friend.

Clifford What right does this nigger have to fire me?

He shakes John off.

John It's OK. He's upset. It's understandable.

Andrew Firstly he is not a 'nigger', his name is John. Secondly John, it's not understandable, it's unforgivable. And lastly Clifford, if I remember correctly you were never hired. You were never *hired*, Clifford.

The crashing sound of a subway train terminates the scene. The sound crescendos alarmingly, finally fading as the train recedes and lights come up to reveal:

2. Avenue X. A Subway Station.

*The station is at ground level. A black metal wall
obliterated by graffiti. Untouched is a sign reading
'AVENUE X' in pure white letters on a black ground.*
   *Anne has just gotten off the train. She's alone on the
platform. Simon appears. They look at each other.*

Simon This has cost me a token. (*to pass through the
turnstile*)

Anne Couldn't you 've jumped it?

Simon There's a camera.

   ,

This has cost me a token and I'm not even going
anywhere. (*faint laugh*)

   ,

(*expressionless – as if reading from a piece of paper, but
staring at her*) 'I'm not coming back Simon I'm never
coming back I have my own room money people who
are because they are interested in me perhaps I want to
be corrupted perhaps I need to be corrupted I've spent
my life with you behind a steel door.'
   But here you are. Have you been waiting long?

Anne I just got off the train. No.

Simon The F.

Anne It doesn't mean I've come back.

   ,

D'you like my dress?

Simon Why?

The blind taxi driver appears and passes along the platform to the exit using a stick. He pays no attention to Anne.

Anne Excuse me. Can I help you? Don't I know you? Can I help? Excuse me.

He's gone.

Simon You know that guy?

Anne He drives a cab. Yes.

,

Simon A cab?

Anne What d'you think? (*of the dress which she spins to exhibit*)

,

D'you think I'm a victim?

Simon What of?

Anne (*shrugs*) You?

Simon This has cost me a token, Anne. I'm taking time off work. What do you *want*?

Anne I want you to hurt someone.

,

It's so hot I nearly stayed on the train. I thought I'd stay on to Coney Island, maybe ride the Cyclone, d'you remember how I / *screamed*?

Simon *What*?

,

Anne How I screamed.

,

354

Simon I fixed the shower.

Anne Did you? Was it the washer?

Simon I changed the washer.

Anne That's cool.

Simon It still drips.

Anne Uh-huh.

Simon But not so much.

Anne Simon?

She takes his head in her hands.

Simon Nice dress.

Anne Thank you.

Simon Hurt someone.

Anne Yes.

Simon I have a lot of work.

Anne Are they making you work too hard?

Simon I'm always digging up the sidewalk. It numbs my hands . . .

Anne Your poor hands . . . (*She takes his hands.*)

Simon . . . so I can't grip things.

,

I was doing the dishes and I dropped a glass in the sink.

Anne Did it smash?

Simon Of course it smashed.

Anne I'm sorry.

Simon Of course it smashed. A shard cut me. The sink was full of blood. I can't grip things, Anne.

Anne But it was wet. It slipped.

Simon I felt sick. I hate blood.

Anne I know you do.

Simon And it was the glass Adam gave us.

Anne Did Adam give us a glass?

Simon When we were married, yes.

Anne I don't recall that glass. Are you / *sure*.

Simon Well now it's smashed.

Anne Adam your father? *That* Adam?

Simon Yes, it was engraved.

,

It had our initials on it.

Anne Adam your father gave us an engraved glass?

Simon (When we were married, yes.) I mean I possess a skill, but they have me laboring, Anne. They make me dig like an animal.

Anne Why's that?

Simon I don't know.

,

I don't know. *Ask* them.

Anne It was only a glass, Simon. I remember that glass. It was just a glass out of the bar.

Simon It was not 'only a glass'.

Anne The initials weren't even ours.

Simon It was not 'only a glass'.

Anne Everything breaks.

Simon I refuse to believe that.

Anne (Everything *we* ever had. Cups. The shower.)

Simon I fixed the shower.

Anne Well everything else.

Simon I fixed the shower, Anne, and I know you hate because you've always hated and despised my family.

Anne That's not what I said.

Simon You hate them because they're good. They're simple. They're not interested in the *unknown*. They don't want – no – to break – like you – to break away or to burrow like you – no – to burrow into themselves like you into the dirt inside of themselves because we all have – yes good fine – we all have that dirt, Anne. I've burrowed into the city and I know it goes because yes it goes down, the city goes down as far maybe farther than it goes *up*. Down down down it goes, which is why we must stay pure, Anne, and good. Why we must look *up*. Life is a gift transmitted from one family to another, not a waste-product to be sent for analysis. You do not check into a hotel to reveal to strangers what goes on behind a private door. You do not reveal to strangers what goes on between *us*.

Anne Nothing *has* gone on between us, Simon.

,

Simon What did you mean: 'hurt'?

Anne And besides I have a lover.

'

Someone who loves me.

'

Simon Is he the one?

'

I fixed the shower, Anne.

Anne I know you did.

> *They look at each other.*

3. The Japanese Restaurant.

Faint music. Wine on the table. Andrew alone, brooding. Waitress appears.

Waitress Are you ready to order?

> *Silence.*

Andrew What sort of music is this?

Waitress It's Japanese music.

Andrew It doesn't sound Japanese.

'

Can it be turned off?

Waitress I'm sorry?

Andrew The Japanese music. Can it be / turned off?

Waitress I don't know, sir.

'

I could *ask*.

Andrew (Leave it.)

Waitress Most people like the Japanese music, but I could ask.

Andrew No. Leave it.

,

Is life very different in Japan?

Waitress I'm from Brooklyn.

Andrew OK.

Waitress Would you like to order now?

Andrew I'm waiting for my wife.

Waitress Of course.

Andrew Why don't you sit down?

Waitress I can't sit down.

Andrew But would you like to?

Waitress Not really, no.

,

Andrew (*taking out card*) Listen . . . it's quite possible that we could use you for something. We're always looking out for new material, ideas.

She looks at the card and puts it back on the table.

Waitress I don't want to be used, thank you.

Andrew Uh-huh? I thought that's why people waited tables – to be discovered.

Waitress I don't want to be discovered.

Andrew Well that is your right.

Waitress OK?

Andrew OK.

They laugh quietly together.
Jennifer arrives.

Jennifer I'm late. *I'm* sorry. Did you order for me?

Andrew I didn't know what you'd want.

Jennifer (He didn't know what I'd want.) Don't I always have K? I'll have K.

,

Andrew?

Andrew What? Yes. Sorry. The same.

Waitress goes. Jennifer pours herself wine and drinks, scrutinising Andrew who continues to brood.

Jennifer Defending her in front of John I was so *embarrassed.*

,

Andrew Would you call this music Japanese?

Jennifer I've been talking to him for hours, Andrew. (What music?) Literally for hours. *Calming* him. There *is* no music.

The music has indeed stopped.

Calming him, Andrew.

,

Andrew I'm going, Jennifer.

Jennifer *I* see. Good. Yes. Go. I've never seen him so mad. He threatened to withdraw everything, the finance, his *name.*

,

Well aren't you going?

He averts his eyes.

The truth is Andrew is that you will never go. Go where? With whom? With Anne? Go with Anne is that the idea? who is at most half your age and in all likelihood mentally (judging by her behavior today) deficient and what? meet her parents in the Lucky Throw?

Andrew (That's not her parents, that's / his.)

Jennifer Have *babies*? Move into the *suburb*? Barbecue a pig on the fourth of *July*? Put up your / *flag*?

Andrew That's not the only alternative.

Jennifer Fine. Go.

Andrew makes no move. Waitress appears with dishes.

Waitress I got them to stop the music.

Andrew (Thank you.)

Waitress goes.

Jennifer Are you *crying*?

He averts his eyes. Jennifer begins to eat.

I worry about you, Andrew.

She continues to eat, choosing her moment.

John said something very interesting. He said, 'What if there is no such man?'

Andrew looks at her.

Exactly. 'What if there is no such man?' What if Anne is lying? Because John can't come to terms with what she

361

says. He doesn't find any truth there. The man she describes is too weird, he is too weird Andrew to be plausible. And to 've *married* him? To 've experienced those humiliations day after day? Well Nicky was right. It's not believable. There is no man. There is just Anne and her imagination. The hood? The tape? The young trees? (*She continues to eat.*) She has invented those things in order to exploit us. You're not eating. Here.

> *She holds up some food for him to eat. He doesn't move. She eats it herself.*

Incidentally, you may like to know she's gone. Yes. She checked out of the hotel. (I guess it was inevitable.)

Andrew Anne is lying?

Jennifer They showed me her room. It's full of dead flowers. Your eyes are red. You look / terrible.

Andrew She's lying?

Jennifer Had you never thought of that?

,

(Yes she checked out right after the meeting. Her account has been closed naturally. The fax / has gone out.)

Andrew Let's leave.

Jennifer Leave.

Andrew Yes. Come with me. I have to get out.

Jennifer Keep your voice down. What d'you mean, get out?

Andrew Get out. Now.

Jennifer Out of the restaurant? Andrew?

Andrew I feel sick.

Jennifer Are you sick? What is it?

Andrew I need some air. (I *believed* in her.)

Jennifer You *have* some air. This room is full / of air.

Andrew I want to go. I want to leave.

Jennifer Right now?

Andrew I want to leave the restaurant, yes.

,

Jennifer There's no air out there, Andrew. Out there it's eighty degrees.

Andrew I want to *get out*, Jennifer.

Waitress (*coming over*) Is he alright?

Jennifer He feels a little sick. I think we should have the check.

  Waitress goes.

Andrew I need to be outside (*He stands.*)

Jennifer I'll call a cab. D'you need the bathroom?

Andrew I want to walk.

Jennifer *Can* you walk?

Andrew Of course I can walk.

Jennifer Is this about Anne?

Andrew Yes it's about Anne. Of course it's about Anne.

Jennifer Forget about her Andrew. She's gone. (Those flowers, they were completely dry, they / crumbled.)

Andrew I'm frightened.

Jennifer We closed the account. Don't be frightened.

Andrew I believed in her.

Jennifer We all believed in her.

Andrew I *loved* her.

Jennifer So did we all love her. But it doesn't affect the work. The work's unaffected.

Andrew She lied to us? To me? Are you sure?

Jennifer In fact the buzz is good. Already the buzz is good. John ended up being very / positive.

Andrew I need to be outside.

Jennifer (*looking for the waitress*) Where is that girl? Did you have a jacket? Is this jacket yours?

Andrew I don't know.

Jennifer It looks like yours.

Andrew Is it?

Jennifer (*helping him into the jacket*) You need me, Andrew. You need me to help you.

Andrew I know.

Jennifer You're too easily deceived. You lack insight.

Andrew I know. I'm sorry. She's a bitch.

Jennifer John opened my eyes. A bitch (that's right) in heat, Andy.

Andrew I feel humiliated.

Jennifer You have been humiliated.

Andrew It's frightening here.

Jennifer Where *is* everyone? Waitress?

Andrew She *sat* here. She sat at this table.

Jennifer Waitress?

Andrew She spoke.

Jennifer The account's closed, Andrew. It's over.

4. Canal Street and Broadway. The Sidewalk.

Clifford is selling dishes as at the beginning of the play. A Mad Woman is picking through the items. In a corner, unseen by Clifford, Anne and Simon are watching.

Woman My kid has diarrhoea. He's had diarrhoea for three days.

Clifford Uh-huh?

Woman Isn't that something? Three days of diarrhoea?

Clifford Quite something.

Woman D'you have anything for diarrhoea?

Clifford You need a drugstore. All I / have is –

Woman (*picks up a bottle*) What's in this bottle?

Clifford It's silver polish.

Woman But what's *in* it.

Clifford Silver polish is in it.

Woman But what's in the polish?

Clifford I'm sorry.

Woman You think because I'm poor I'm ignorant? That I would poison my child? But what I'm saying is is there are things *in* things. You say 'this is polish' but inside the polish may be something good for diarrhoea just as in many *medicines* there is a poison. How come you have silver polish anyway?

Clifford It belonged to my mother.

Woman Did she polish silver or was it polished for her?

Clifford The latter, I suppose. (That's very astute.)

Woman 'The latter I suppose.' You have a very English way of speaking, you know that? Was your mother English?

Clifford She was from Europe.

Woman And she brought all this silver? – and this china? – is that Limoges?

Simon Is that him?

Anne Yes. Go on.

Clifford It was a wedding present. Yes.

Woman I'll take the polish. How much is it?

Clifford Fifty cents – but don't give it to a child.

Woman D'you have children?

Clifford No.

Woman Then you know nothing. What do you know? You could have children. You could have grandchildren. Then you might understand.

    Simon comes over.

Clifford My work has always come first.

Woman What work is that?

Simon Excuse me.

Woman Well I'm pleased to 've met you. (*She moves away.*)

Simon Excuse me.

Clifford Do we know each other?

The Woman sits on the ground and begins to drink the polish. Simon takes out the fork.

Simon I have a complaint about this fork.

Clifford A complaint?

,

I remember. I sold you this for five. What's wrong with it?

Simon Look at these tines.

Clifford What tines? What is a tine?

Simon The prongs. Look at them.

Clifford The prongs are called tines? *That's* interesting. I didn't / know that.

Simon Didn't you know that? I thought words were your trade. Feel them. Yes.

Clifford They're like needles. They shouldn't be / like that.

Simon Exactly. I sharpened them on a stone.

,

Clifford Well you've done a very foolish thing. You've ruined a good fork.

Simon Don't call me a fool.

Clifford It was a good fork. It had a history.

Simon I have a complaint.

Clifford *You* did that to the fork, young man. I sold you in good faith. Now I'm sorry / if you've –

367

Simon The complaint is not on my behalf. It's on behalf of my wife.

Clifford Now listen. I don't *know* your wife

Simon I think that you do.

Clifford Why did you do this to a good fork?

Simon I think that you do. I think that you defiled her honor.

Clifford You use some very strange words. Now listen –

Simon You looked at her. You spied on her. You defiled her.

Clifford I don't know your wife.

Simon I think that you do.

Clifford catches sight of Anne.

Clifford Listen . . . I'm sorry about the fork. Please choose another.

Simon I don't want another.

Clifford Look, take back your five. Take back ten.

Simon I don't want back my five.

Clifford So what do you want?

Anne DO IT.

Simon (*matter of fact*) Revenge.

Clifford Listen, why don't we –

Simon stabs the fork into Clifford's eye.

Anne TWIST IT.

Simon twists the fork, lets it fall.

The other eye. Simon!

As Simon backs away Anne rushes forward and stabs the fork into Clifford's other eye as he lies on the ground. Immediately a siren sounds. Simon and Anne run off. The Mad Woman starts to pick through Clifford's things and drop them into a bag.

Jennifer and Andrew appear on their way from the restaurant to the office. They've not seen Simon and Anne. The Mad Woman picks up her bag and makes off, knocking against Jennifer.

Jennifer Has something happened here?

Woman His things. He asked me to take care of his things.

The Woman slips away. The siren sounds. Jennifer hangs back, but Andrew approaches Clifford. Neither recognises him.

Jennifer Has something happened here? Andrew? Don't touch him.

Clifford Help me.

Jennifer Don't touch him, Andrew. You're sick.

Clifford Help me. I've been robbed.

Jennifer My husband's sick. I'm sorry. He can't help. Andrew. Come *on*. This neighbourhood's / not *safe*.

Clifford (*turning to Jennifer*) I *know* you. I know your voice.

Andrew Clifford? Are you Clifford?

Clifford I *know* you. Who *are* you?

Andrew Who did this to you?

Jennifer You're sick, Andrew. Come / *on*.

Clifford A man. It was a man.

369

Andrew A man did this to you? What man?

Clifford It was her husband.

Jennifer This is not our problem, Andrew.

Andrew Whose husband?

Jennifer This is not our *problem*.

Andrew Whose husband?

Clifford Who *are* you? I *know* you. Help me. It's dark.

Jennifer eases Andrew away. They go.

It's dark. Who did I offend?

Blackout.

Act Four

1. TriBeCa. The Empty Office.

*In silence a group of formally dressed men and women
file in until they fill most of the space. They don't speak.
They wait.*

*Then, in this order, enter Jennifer, Nicky and lastly
John, also wearing formal clothes, jewelry. The crowd
begins to applaud on seeing Jennifer, the enthusiasm
increasing with Nicky, at maximum on John.*

*The applause goes on and on as the three take up
positions: Jennifer and Nicky at the back of the crowd,
John at the front, facing them. Finally John, smiling,
gestures for silence.*

*The mood is happy and relaxed. The crowd reacts
to John's speech with unforced good humor and
enthusiasm.*

John What is the meaning of success?

The answer, my friends, is nothing.

Nothing that is, unless it be success deserved, success
merited.

Tonight we have merited that success.

Applause.

Let me begin – a rhetorical device because I have of
course already begun –

Laughter.

Let me begin with a word or two about Anne – the real
Anne.

Stillness.

371

Art is nothing without life – and life is what Anne brought to us – *true* life – with all its fragility, inconsistency and banality – and yet at the same time – in Anne – both beauty and strength. This is the room, the same room, in which she told us her story and wept.

Stillness.

Our only regret is that she was not able to understand the process of transformation by which life becomes art – a process in which, at times, truth must be laid on a Procrustean bed and cut here and there until it fits. (Not too messily we hope.)

Laughter.

Talking of Anne brings me – a little too conveniently I admit –

Laughter.

– but brings me nevertheless to Nicky. To Nicole. Nicole.

He extends his hand. To applause, Nicky makes her way to the front and takes John's hand.

When I first joined this project a year ago, Nicky here was working on reception. She was answering *telephones.*

Laughter.

I'm quite serious. Wasn't that so?

Nicky That's what I did.

John That's what she did. That is indeed what she did and none of us at that time could've foreseen the stroke of genius (my own as it happens) –

Laughter.

– which would result in her – untrained – inexperienced as she then was – in her being chosen to play Anne. But –

as you have all seen tonight – she does not 'play' Anne, she *is* Anne. She inhabits Anne. At certain moments she is more Anne than Anne herself.

Nicky (Thank you.)

John (It's true.) (*gesture*) Nicole.

More applause for Nicky.

Now I know you're all anxious to eat, to dance. Yes. I see it in your eyes. A certain restlessness.

Laughter.

But tonight would not be complete if I failed to mention the two facilitators of this project. Jennifer. And Andrew.

To applause Jennifer makes her way to the front.

Andrew? Where are you? We seem to 've lost Andrew.

Laughter.

Jennifer (He's not well. He's lying down.)

John (He's lying down?) Andrew is lying down. What've you been doing to him, Jen.

Laughter. Jennifer forces a smile. John takes her hand and waits for stillness.

A year ago what was this project? It was nothing. It was a page.

Jennifer (Less than a page.)

John It was less – exactly – than a page. But their tenacity, their violent need to create, transformed that page.

Stillness.

Jen and I go back a long way, a long long way.

Jennifer (Not too far, John.)

Laughter. She forces a smile.

John Not too far – of course not too far – but far enough. Far enough to be part of a time when we seriously believed our actions would bring about – what Jen? revolution? peace? (fuck knows quite frankly).

Laughter.

But that idealism –

Jennifer (We weren't quite so vague, John.)

John (Not quite so vague but vague enough.) That idealism has stayed with us. It has stayed with us in our art. Now, it's fashionable to believe, my friends, that art changes nothing. But on the contrary, what I say to you is that art changes *everything* –

Tremendous applause.

(*over applause*) It is the enduring reflection of our transient selves. It is what makes us *real*.

The applause continues until John gestures for silence.

And now, I believe – yes – my speech has ended.

Laughter.

There is food. There is wine.

Nicky (A band.)

John Even a band. Thank you all.
(*He gestures to the door.*) Enjoy.

The crowd files out.
    Nicky is first to move. She sits in a chair. She lowers her head.

Nicky Why do I feel so tense? John?

*John comes behind her and begins to massage her
shoulders, which are naked.
Jennifer doesn't move.
The massage goes on in concentration and silence to
Jennifer's increasing discomfort.
Finally, without stopping, John speaks.*

John How is Andrew?

,

Should you see him?

Jennifer He may be asleep. He often sleeps.

Jennifer lights a cigarette. Massage continues.

John Jennifer is smoking. When did you start smoking /
Jennifer?

Jennifer He just lies down and sleeps.

John Wake him.

,

Rouse him.

Faint laugh from Nicky.

Or is that no longer possible?

,

He's a weak man.

Nicky He's not asleep.

,

Jennifer I'm sorry?

Nicky Andrew. He's not asleep.

John He's a weak man. Not only does he have many weaknesses, but he gives in to them all. Perhaps that's his / charm.

Jennifer Have you been in to him?

John Because he does have charm – he can charm people away – *oh* yes.

Jennifer Have you been into the room?

Massage continues.

Nicky What room?

Jennifer The room he was sleeping in. (Are you doing this / deliberately?)

John To think that when she married him I was crushed. Utterly. / (*faint laugh*)

Nicky He was never asleep. He was not *in* the room. He's gone. (*to John*) Really? Were you?

Jennifer Where?

Nicky To Anne. He's gone to Anne.

Jennifer How can he 've gone to Anne?

John ('Gone to Anne.' It doesn't surprise me. That's what I mean by / weakness.)

Nicky He made me get out the old file. He wanted her address. That's where he's gone.

Jennifer And you gave him the file? You let him go? You *said* nothing? When *was* this?

Nicky I'm no longer your servant, Jennifer.

Nicky and John exchange a look and quiet laugh which confirm Jennifer's exclusion. Jennifer perceives this and leaves the room.

(*Calls after her.*) The file's still out if you want it. It's green.

In silence the massage continues.

Nicky Did you mean what you said?

John What did I say?

Nicky Don't you recall? You made a speech, a great speech. John?

She twists her head round to look up at him, but he stares ahead, continuing the massage.

John I recall nothing.

,

D'you hear that sound?

,

Nicky I don't hear any sound.

John It's the elevator. It's Jen going down to the street. Down down down she goes. To the street.

,

Nicky I don't hear it.

John Listen. (*He stills his hands.*)

Stillness. She listens. A very faint whine, as of an elevator, becomes audible. But as the light begins to dim on Nicky and John, the sound develops into the roar of a subway train which finally recedes as before to introduce:

377

2. Avenue X. Anne and Simon's Apartment.

Anne is alone. She occupies exactly the same position as Nicky in the previous scene, sitting in a chair. However, unlike Nicky, she is tied to the chair and her mouth is taped shut. In the distance, intermittently, a dog barks.

Close to Anne's face a battered fan slowly oscillates.

She wears the same dress as in Act Three. It has grown ragged.

A long silence.

Andrew appears in the room, dressed in his formal clothes.

He goes to Anne.

She makes no sound. He unties her. He carefully peels the tape from her mouth.

She wets her lips. No other reaction.

Andrew Anne?

Anne Who are you?

'

How did you get in here?

Andrew The door's not locked.

Anne That's a steel door. It's always locked.

'

Always.

Andrew It's Andrew.

Anne Andrew?

'

Anne You don't own that dog do you, Andrew? I worry about that dog. It sounds distressed.

378

Andrew starts to look around the room.

You know *I'm* sorry but this is wrong. It's wrong to walk into someone's apartment like this. What are you looking for? We don't have anything. Do we look like we have things? Why are you dressed like that? Do I know you?

Andrew Is there somebody here?

Anne We've *been* robbed. A while back. There's nothing left to take.

Andrew picks up a piece of dark fabric.

Andrew What is this?

Anne A hood. It belongs to my husband.

Andrew examines the hood. The dog is heard.

I'm sorry but it has no value. Listen, if you own that dog why don't you feed it or exercise it or *care* for it / in some way?

Andrew (*discards hood*) I thought you'd like to know it's a great success, Anne.

Anne What is?

Andrew Your life.

Anne I don't follow. A success?

Andrew Yes.

Anne Well. OK. Perhaps. I have enough to eat. I have my health. (*faint laugh*) Also I'm pregnant, so please – please don't hurt me.

Andrew You don't look pregnant.

Anne I even quit smoking. I used to smoke. I quit.

Andrew (*hardly suppressing his anger*) Why don't you move?

Anne I beg your pardon?

Andrew (*as before*) Why don't you *move*? Get out of that chair? I've untied you. That door isn't steel. It's not even *locked*.

Anne (*calmly*) Move where? *I'm* sorry – this is my home. This is my chair. Why don't *you* move? Why don't you get the fuck out? (Dressed like that, poking about, Jesus Christ this is *my* / apartment.) (*She looks away from him, rubbing her wrists.*)

Andrew I want you to come with me before he gets back.

Anne Before who gets back? What if I don't want / to come?

Andrew The man.

Anne What man? D'you mean my husband?

Andrew Do you have a husband?

Anne I'm pregnant. Of course I have a husband.

Andrew Simon.

Anne Yes.

Andrew Where is he? Where is Simon?

Anne Don't you believe me?

Andrew Where is Simon?

Anne Are you one of his friends? I never meet his friends. He prefers to go out alone. He tells me all about them, though.

Andrew Please, Anne

Anne There's Joel – Joel's gay but he's very very funny – and Max of course – and Holly who's just had a baby girl. Then there's Ross who works for Adam behind the bar. *His* cousin's a police officer. Which one are you? Are you Joel?

Andrew My name is Andrew.

Anne He's never mentioned you.

Andrew I'm not one of his / friends.

Anne I used to really crave to go out. My dream was to go through that door. But now I see how wrong I was to crave and how right he was to keep me in. Because last time we went out together we did something really really terrible. (*Lowers voice.*) You won't believe this, but we put out a man's eyes. (*Faint laugh. She continues to rub her wrists.*)

Andrew How d'you mean, 'put them out'?

Anne Right out of his head. How else out?

She turns and looks straight at him. Her tone changes.

I know who you are.
I think you should leave.

Simon appears. He's drinking from a bottle of beer in a paper bag, as when first seen.
He looks briefly at Andrew and Anne.

Simon I need to take a shower.

Anne Is it hot out?

Simon It's still hot.

Anne What time is it?

Simon It's two a.m.

Anne You're back early.

,

This is the man owns the dog.

Simon What dog?

Anne The dog we always hear, Simon.

Simon (Pleased to meet you.) I never hear a dog, Anne.

Anne He never hears it. He imagines this neighbourhood is peaceful.

Simon What sort of dog do you have?

Andrew I don't have a dog. I don't own a dog. I'm *sorry*. That's not why I'm here.

Simon Uh-huh?

,

In that case Anne is / mistaken.

Anne How was Joel?

Simon Joel wasn't there tonight. Why is he dressed like that?

Andrew My name is Andrew.

Simon In fact that's why we left. It's not so much fun without Joel. Andrew? I see. Is it?

Andrew I want Anne to come with me.

Simon Would 'Andrew' like a beer? What do you drink, Andrew?

Andrew I want her to leave. / Now.

Simon Anne, why don't you get Andrew a beer?

'

Perhaps you don't drink. That's very wise. My wife is pregnant. She's given up – haven't you Anne? – tobacco *and* alcohol. In fact the last time she drank / which was approximately

Anne (Please stop, Simon.)

Simon twelve months ago (stop? why?) the last time she drank she was raped by a complete stranger.

Anne I was not raped / Simon.

Simon Raped by a complete stranger, Andrew. This is in we're talking a respectable apartment on the Upper West Side where they have servants and candles and if they look east they can see the Park.

'

Yes.

Anne (I was not raped.)

Simon So perhaps you don't drink. Do you drink?

'

Why don't you sit / down?

Andrew Anne, we have / to go.

Simon D'you see – Andrew – how the colour's come back to her hair – and to her eyes? (Go? I don't think so.) Look at her eyes. They're blue again. Show him your eyes, Anne. D'you see how the light comes from the inside? That's because she eats properly now. No one's trying to feed her in the mouth, Andrew. She eats good fresh things which I cook for her. I shop for her, I cook for her, everything is done for her, isn't it, Anne. Sometimes I *wash* her, I wash her body – isn't that so?

Anne Sometimes he washes me. It's true.

Simon You see? Why don't you sit down?

Anne But I'll wash the baby sometimes, won't I Simon? That is what you said?

Simon Of course you'll wash the baby.

Anne (*faint laugh*) I hate the way their heads flop back.

Simon You have to cradle their heads, Anne. I've told you.

Anne (Yes. OK. Cradle them.) It's kind of scarey. So many things can go wrong. Pregnancy. Delivery. Infancy. Do you have any children?

Simon Nothing will go wrong, Anne. Just cradle his head.

Anne I will take him out sometimes, won't I?

Simon Of course you'll take him out. He has to see the world. The sky. Trees. The young trees.

Anne I'd like to go out.

Simon You can always go out.

Silence.

Andrew Can she go out now?

Silence.

Simon She can always go out, but she chooses not to.

Andrew Why don't you go out, Anne. Get some air.

Anne (*confused*) What? Now? It's late. I . . .

Simon It's just that she chooses not to.

Andrew Yes. Go out now.

Anne I'm not really dressed. I . . .

Simon She doesn't *want* to go out. That's *her* choice.

Anne I'm not really dressed. My hair . . . (*She runs her hand through it.*) Look at it.

,

Perhaps for a few minutes, Simon. May I?

Andrew Go now.

Simon She chooses not to, that's all.

> *Anne hesitates, then moves very slowly away from Simon and towards the way out. She breaks into a run and goes.*

This proves nothing.

> *Offstage, a single shot.*
> *Simon goes out.*
> *A moment passes. Andrew doesn't move.*
> *Jennifer enters, holding the gun.*

Jennifer She *ran* at me. I just *reacted*. Why did she *run*? I *reacted* to that. It's so *threatening* here, Andrew.

> *Stillness.*

She was running *towards* me. *At* me. There's no light, she *appeared*. *Don't* look at me like that. She appeared, it was a reaction.

> *Stillness.*

I've been wandering this lousy project in a state of *total fear*, Andrew. Nothing is *numbered*. *Total fear*. Why did you do this? FUCK this. Are you now HAPPY?

> *She throws down the gun.*
> *Simon enters. He looks at them.*

(*softly*) She ran at me. It was a threat. I reacted.

> *Long silence.*

385

Simon My child.

Jennifer Are you *Simon*?

> *Blackout and simultaneously Clifford's voice calling 'Taxi! Taxi!'*

3. Taxi!

Faint light reveals Clifford calling for a taxi. He's clutching a sheaf of papers. Throughout the scene pages fall from the sheaf and are swept away by a current of air.

> *The taxi driver appears as before.*

Driver Where to?

Clifford Where is this?

Driver 'Where is this?' Don't you know?

Clifford I *think* I know.

Driver Well tell me what you think.

Clifford I think this is Canal Street and Broadway.

Driver I think you're right. I think this is Canal Street. It feels like Canal Street.

Clifford Don't you know? Isn't there / a *sign*?

Driver I've lived in this city all of my life.

Clifford Me too.

Driver That's unusual.

Clifford Yes. D'you think?

Driver Where can I take you?

Clifford Broadway and East Fifty-Second.

Driver There is no such thing.

Clifford But I was given the address.

Driver Well I'm sorry but there is no such thing.

Sheets of paper continue to blow away.

What kind of place is it you want? I could take you to *West* Fifty-Second and Broadway.

Clifford I have to deliver some work.

Driver In the middle of the night.

Clifford Is this the middle of the night?

Driver Certainly.

Clifford I didn't know that.

Driver What kind of work is it?

Clifford A script.

Driver Can't you mail it?

Clifford (*gripping the paper*) Am I losing pages?

Driver A script? You a writer?

Pages continue to blow away.

Driver Listen, why don't I just take you uptown. (A writer, you must have lots of things inside of yourself, *stories.*)

Clifford I need this delivered. I don't want to talk.

Driver I'll take you uptown. Do I have a green light?

Clifford I'm sorry?

Driver Do I have a green / light?

Clifford Are you mocking me? I'm blind. *Look* at me.

Driver I'm not mocking you.

Clifford OK.

Driver Were you blind at birth?

Clifford No.

Driver D'you have a *disease*?

Clifford I don't want to talk.

Driver So I just / drive?

Clifford Just drive. Yes.

  They drive.

Driver May I ask your name?

Clifford (Clifford. Clifford Webb.)

Driver You're not *the* Clifford Webb.

Clifford Yes as a matter of fact yes I am.

Driver (*with joy*) Shit! I have Clifford Webb in my taxi. This is an *honor*, Clifford. Hey . . .

Clifford (Thank you.)

Driver This is a real honor. I wish I could see your face. I hear your name all the time on the radio. Clifford Webb says this. Clifford Webb thinks that. And my wife she watches that show you do on TV.

  They drive.

Clifford What d'you mean, 'see my face'?

Driver She says it is so thought / provoking.

Clifford What d'you mean, 'see my face'? Why can't you see my face?

Driver Listen, you don't want to talk to me, Clifford, and I respect that. Would the radio bother you? Are you trying to *think*?

He turns on the radio.
  Softly, the boogie-woogie heard at the top of Act Three.

Clifford Am I losing pages?

The pages continue to blow away and tumble across the space. The driver clicks his fingers in time with the music.

Driver Let's try taking a right here.

Blast of horn.

Take it easy my friend. I have Clifford Webb in the back of this cab.

He continues to click. The music grows louder. The pages tumble through the air. More frequent horn blasts.

Clifford What d'you mean, 'see my face'? Where is this? Where are we going?

Driver I've no idea, Clifford. But isn't that one of the joys, one of the great joys of this city?

Music up loud.
  Lights fade.
  Music continues as they go into the dark.